THE SPIRIT OF AFRICAN DESIGN

THE SPIRIT OF AFRICAN

by Sharne Algotsson and Denys Davis

DESIGN

written by Yanick Rice Lamb

photographs by George Ross

design by Helene Silverman

Clarkson Potter/Publishers

New York

To Ahmad, Malik, and Vanessa

Text copyright © 1996 by Sharne Algotsson and Denys Davis
Photographs copyright © 1996 by George Ross

Published by Clarkson N. Potter, Inc., 201 East 50th Street, New York, New York 10022.
Member of the Crown Publishing Group.

Random House, Inc. New York, Toronto, London, Sydney, Auckland

http://www.randomhouse.com/

CLARKSON N. POTTER, POTTER, and colophon are trademarks of Clarkson N. Potter, Inc.

Printed in China

Library of Congress Cataloging-in-Publication Data
Algotsson, Sharne.
The spirit of African design / by Sharne Algotsson and Denys Davis.—1st ed.
p.   cm.
Includes index.
1. Decoration and ornament—Africa, Sub-Saharan. 2. Art, Black—Africa, Sub-Saharan.
I. Davis, Denys. II. Title.
NK1488.75.A43 1996
709'.67—dc20   95-12992
CIP

ISBN 0-517-59916-3

10 9 8 7 6 5 4

ACKNOWLEDGMENTS

This project would not have been possible without the help of the many generous people who supported us from beginning to end. In particular we would like to thank our husbands, Jan Algotsson and Anthony Davis, for holding down the fort and keeping our spirits high.

To those who helped in getting this project off the ground, we thank Dr. Frances Powell, Kagler Curtis, Clotye Larsson, Lloyd Remick, Esq., Gladys Carter, Doris and Kelsey Brown, and Jamie Foster-Brown.

To Ethel Williamson, Tahira Amatullah, Warren Robbins, Dr. Harriet Schiffer, Drs. Kariamu and Molefe Welsh-Asante, Professor Wanyandey Songha, Derek Beard, Dr. Theophile Obenga, Tina Swarg, Djibril Diallo, Christopher Owles, and Courtney Kardon, we thank you for your willingness to share your extensive knowledge and provide us with invaluable research material and contacts.

As for the difficult task of finding the many wonderful homes included in our book, it could not have been done successfully without the help of Herman Bigham, Eric Robertson, Phera-lyn Dove, Richard Watson, and Sally Lasdon.

Thank you to Cheryl Levin and Chris Lynn, Michele Weist, Joan Harrington, and Valery Johnson, our creative support team who helped bring our ideas to life. Thanks as well to the many designers and gallery owners: Deborah Cholet, Anthony Fisher, Ignacio Villarrel, Ford Wheeler, Catherine Holt, Mel Fisher, Liz Galbraith, Ephraim Paul, Arthur Meckler, Janet L. Kalter, Al and Janet Sitnik, Steve Harrington, Mary Ann Boxley, Mohammed Mesbahi, Cheryl Riley, Courtney Sloane, Alex Locadia, Maxime de La Falaise, Anje Loock, Alison King, Barbara Lewis, Karen Riggs, Skye Kirby, Lorrie Payne, Barry Durst, Lucille Clark, Teresa McCrae, Saz Zachary, Phile Chionesu, Hillary Blomberg, Jane Krolik, Zumbi Soweto, Derrick Joshua Beard, and Stephanie Zuckerman, whose contributions often provided the finishing touch.

We are truly grateful to our photographer, George Ross, for his magical technique in capturing and enhancing the beauty and character of each home, and for the help of Lewis Bloom, who provided a creative second eye. Additional photographs provided by Christer Algotsson, Pieter Estersohn, Solvi Dos Santos, Oberto Gili, Ahmad Kenya, Yuri Marder, Marie Claire Maison, National Museum of African Art of the Smithsonian Institute, Bob McCarthy, Conde Naste Publications, Herman Miller Inc., the Metropolitan Museum of Art, and Sotheby's were greatly appreciated. And many thanks to our writer, Yanick Rice Lamb, who brought a beautiful sensitivity and understanding to our material.

A special thank-you to the following homeowners: Tahira Amatullah, Armand and Corice Arman, Drs. Kariamu and Molefe Welsh-Asante, Carlos Ascher, Joe Sam and Donna Bellorado, Jack and Helen Bershad, Nina Beskow, Barbara Jane Bullock, Barbara Carter-Mitchell, Stephan Janson, Debbie Johnson, Deborah Johnson, William Karg and Reese Fayde, Margreet and Willem Monster, Richard and Jeanne Presha, Roger Prigent, Cheryl Riley, Warren Robbins, Veronica Robertson, J. R. Sanders, Buster Seccia, Robert Teszar, Carolyn Tyler, Sheryl and Charles Ward, and Maureen Zarember.

We would like to thank our friend Joan Harrington, a graphic artist and illustrator, for creating the handpainted paste paper designs that appear throughout the book. To our book designer Helene Silverman for creating a wonderful marriage of images and words, thank you.

Finally, we extend sincere gratitude to our editor, Annetta Hanna, for her patience and guidance, as well as additional support from Roy Finamore, Howard Klein, Jane Treuhaft, Amy Boorstein, Joan Denman, and Lauren Shakely at Clarkson Potter.

CONTENTS

PREFACE

When we started this book three years ago, our goal was to take traditional African art out of the museum and look at it in the home. We believed this would give many people a great deal of pleasure; we also hoped to inspire a new appreciation for African culture and its influence on the world of art and design. For us, working on this book was a spiritual discovery. In a sense, we didn't choose the project; it chose us. We were led, as if by magic, in this direction by our interests, travels, and backgrounds. Although we had known each other professionally for nearly a decade, it wasn't until we were assigned to work long hours together on a designer's show house that we realized just how much we had in common. Besides sharing strong design backgrounds, we both had grown up with an enriched awareness of African culture. Little did we know the effects of being surrounded by the art collected or created by our families!

In each of our careers, we journeyed around the world through design. Along the way, we witnessed a dramatic shift: style became less prescriptive and more reflective of how we actually live. One example of this shift is the growing number of people who are infusing their lives with African flavor. The explosion of interest in African style—and the growth in resources to feed this interest—is tremendous. Witness the new galleries and shops specializing in African art, the variety of excursions to the continent, the music in the air, and the increasing use of African motifs on everything from evening wear, layettes, and bomber jackets to china, wallpaper, and sheets. We're excited by these developments as well as intrigued by the information and images that we unlocked during our own pilgrimage to the past. Most of all, we're delighted to share our findings, our expertise, and our profound enjoyment of African style.

Despite its visual impact upon modern art, African design has often been underrepresented and underappreciated in Western cultural surveys. Far too often, it is presented in simplistic anthropological terms as being primitive, tribal, or ethnic. This greatly downplays its stylistic complexity and importance. African design is more than masks, zebra skins, and Kente cloth. Its visual impact upon and its kinship with sophisticated formal trends come through in all sorts of less obvious ways. Note, for example, the parallels between the sculptural forms of African stools and modern curvilinear furniture.

Although Africa is a vast continent with a mélange of cultures, ecological systems, and creative perspectives, there are commonalities that transcend its many internal borders. Functional integrity, the graphic use of spiritual symbolism, and a focus on organic elements are constants, from Niger to South Africa, Morocco to Tanzania. For instance, whether textiles are woven by Ethiopian men in East Africa or Berber women in North Africa, the colors hold social or ritual significance.

We hope this book will help you sort through the various elements of African style. We are not attempting to re-create here the traditional African home, whatever or wherever that may be. Rather, we have chosen to showcase homes around us (including our own), sharing their creative use, both functional and aesthetic, of African and African-inspired art and design. We hope you will enjoy visiting these homes as much as we did, and that you will turn to this book not only as a resource of inventive designs but also as a rewarding guide to creating your own interpretations of African style. The possibilities are unlimited!

SHARNE ALGOTSSON AND DENYS DAVIS

INTRODUCTION

For many people, living with African artifacts creates a spiritual connection to the continent—it's the next best thing to being there. That's the way Robert Teszar, a New York design stylist, feels about his generously proportioned, wood-carved Senufo bed from the Ivory Coast. "When I'm away, I can imagine it coming to life and walking around the apartment," he explains. Teszar considers his design choices to be very personal, while at the same time encompassing a connection to many traditional aspects of African culture. Here in this book, we look at African art and design through the same lens, celebrating both idiosyncratic tastes and culturally meaningful choices.

African art reflects the diverse societies of men and women who have lived off this rich land, designing their objects to include both function and symbolism. It evokes a time when fabric dyes were derived from plants, earth, and minerals; when cloth was produced from the pounding of tree bark; and when wooden objects were carved with rudimentary tools. As the world grows increasingly complicated and we move ever farther from any link to our own traditional ways, it makes sense perhaps that we are drawn to the qualities manifest in this time-less art: simplicity, natural elegance, symbolism, functionality, and craftsmanship.

While Africa, as a source of visual inspiration, still possesses a wealth of artistic integrity and historical imagery, it is nevertheless a continent in transition. New design influences and contemporary art forms are constantly emerging. Vast numbers of people are leaving their villages for sprawling cities like Accra, Lagos, Dakar, Abidjan, and Rabat, never to return. As peoples all over the globe grapple with similar changes, we can examine the effects of this massive social transition on art traditions throughout Africa. What has been forever lost? What is being reincarnated in new ways? Some of the answers can be found in our book.

Taking these influences back to our own continent, we extend an invitation to visit a variety of living spaces, courtesy of hosts who have graciously offered to share their creative links to the past and present of Africa. Among the homeowners here are historians, photographers, artists, stylists, art collectors, dealers, television anchors, museum administrators, educators, decorators, and designers of furniture, fashion, interiors, and exhibitions. Each of their homes is unique, with interiors that suggest wonderful stories, reflecting their owners' love for Africa, its art and design, its land and its peoples.

Some homes contain noteworthy collections of West and Central African masks and sculpture, assemblages that have been years in the making. Other homes feature less formal collections of art, chosen for their individual design, craftsmanship, or history, with a focus on interior decoration. Utilitarian pieces, including chairs, stools, fabric, carpets, pottery, and basketry, abound, and are a part of everyday life, just as in Africa. There are European interpretations of African art, such as an impressive collection of 19th-century Empire furniture; at the opposite end of the spectrum are the avant-garde African-inspired pieces of furniture designed by such contemporary designers as Alex Locadia, Cheryl Riley, and Courtney Sloane.

These homes speak of the exotic elegance of textiles, the radical simplicity of sculpture, and the intricate craftsmanship of objects found in Africa. They tell us about the continent, and at the same time they offer a new dimension to the design of our own living space, whether it's a studio apartment or a palatial estate. The individuals featured here not only share their ideas and solutions for decorating contemporary living spaces with traditional African art and design, they also express a very special attitude toward their homes—an African state of mind, one could call it.

AFRICAN ART AND DESIGN: BEYOND CATEGORY

In many ways, African art and design defies a single label or definition. Its creativity is inspired by a land of contrasting images, ranging from lush rain forests to sun-parched savannahs, from extreme poverty to extraordinary grandeur. It combines the obvious and the sublime, the primal and the sophisticated, the traditional and the progressive. African design embodies simplicity and complexity at once. Its sculptural styles alone number in the hundreds, and while this spectacular art is decorative, its ornamentation in general evolves either from spiritual symbols or from functional requirements.

Trying to define African art would be as impossible a task as trying to define European art and design. Just as Europe is made up of many nations with divergent histories, religious traditions, political structures, languages, and aesthetics—the works of a Renaissance Dutch painter are far removed from those of a Venetian—the same applies to art and design in Africa, a continent of more than fifty nations containing one-tenth of the world's population. This is especially true since Africans regard themselves first as Hausa, Berber, Fulani, Turkana, Kikuyu, or as members of any one of the other nine hundred or so ethnic groups on the continent; it is through their ethnic identity that they define themselves. The Yoruba, for example, are one of Africa's largest ethnic groups and most prolific art producers. They reside primarily in Nigeria, Benin, and Togo, but they share a rich art culture that transcends national borders— their style is unmistakably Yoruba.

THE NATURAL WORLD AS INSPIRATION

Nature plays a pivotal role in the character of African style. For example, sources of inspiration can come from the continent's deserts—the Sahara, the world's largest, and the Namib or the Kalihari—as well as from the Zairian rain forest and the grasslands of Kenya. Similarly, animals are vitally important to the continent's ideology and folklore, and so lions, snakes, fish, insects, turtles, giraffes, zebras, and antelopes are a constant theme in African art. While their shapes and patterns have at times been overused to the point of becoming visual clichés, these animals serve as timeless examples of the enrichment of Africa's art through its wildlife.

Year after year, in one part of Africa or another, a struggle with nature is being waged, with

survival in the balance. Many African cultures have believed that there are powers in such natural elements as trees, animals, rocks, and rivers that determine the outcome of this struggle. In the belief system known as animism, every occurrence—even the faintest buzz of a bee—can be traced to the spirit world. When things go well, it is believed that the spirits are rewarding human

beings with favors. When things go badly, the spirits are punishing people for the errors of their ways. Since the spirits have great power, they must be respected and placated, giving humans some degree of influence over the wrath of nature by means of prayer, ceremonies of worship, and the creation of objects such as sculpture and masks. And as inspiration for this work, there's no stronger source than nature, which determines almost everything in daily life, from the availability of materials to the use of colors, textures, and imagery. Because nature is so much a part of African life, there is evident a special kinship between the physical world of objects, natural or man-made, and the spiritual well-being of human beings.

WHAT IS AFRICAN STYLE?

African style means hands-on design, requiring from the start imagination and resourcefulness. In establishing criteria for this book, we have taken our cue from African artisans, who combine natural resources with their own creativity to produce the intriguingly beautiful art for which Africa is known. In this book, we explore how to integrate African art into every aspect of the home—furniture, textiles, surfaces, windows and walls, beds and bathrooms, kitchens, and even the garden. The innovative use of traditional painting techniques, for example, provides a dramatic way to transform any area or object. But to accurately capture the African spirit, these patterns, such as the surface designed for a West African drum stand on page 116, should have both a free style and an asymmetrical quality: that is part of their beauty. Several of the homes featured in these pages were skillfully painted by trained

west africa

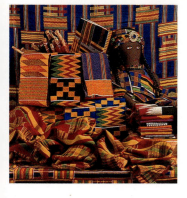

east africa

artists; others were decorated by dedicated amateurs, but they all strive for this sense of authenticity.

African style also offers lots of room for play, both visually and emotionally. Diverse feelings are conveyed, for example, through Moroccan pastels, bold South African primaries, or Tanzanian earth tones. This is a style both attached to the present and appreciative of the historical legacy of African imagery. The intertwining histories of North Africa, the sub-Sahara, and the western, eastern, and southern regions of the continent all come together in African style, yet there is still plenty of room for contemporary Western influences.

NEW LOOK WITH A DISTINGUISHED PAST

The love of art and design has flourished in Africa for centuries. Artistic images have ranged from simple, almost abstract forms to extremely realistic and finely detailed renderings. At various times, however, many Westerners have found it hard to believe that Africans could possess such an extensive artistic repertoire. Some, in fact, have suggested that the realistic images found in Africa were surely created by people from Europe or elsewhere, since African art was believed to be "primitive." We can attribute these misconceptions to a lack of understanding of African culture and history, as well as to personal biases.

In reality, the earliest documented African art and household furnishings date back to 3100 B.C., more than five thousand years ago. While many of these pieces are only fragmented remains found in tombs and pyramids, they nevertheless demonstrate that the ancient societies of the Nile Valley were quite advanced, with artistic sensitivity, cherished traditions, and an

upper class accustomed to comfort and luxury. The Nok culture of Nigeria also has a rich history of artistic skill and traditional techniques. Many exquisite examples of their jewelry and terra-cotta sculptures from 500 B.C. have survived intact, a testimony to the craftsmanship of the time.

Africa has a long tradition of textile art as well. Textile production has been documented to date back more than five thousand years, based on the carbon dating of cloth produced by the Tellem people and found in the caves of Bandiagara, in what is now Mali. In the 1730s, a Danish factor who visited the court of the Asante king Opokuware I in Kumasi, the capital of the Asante confederacy in Ghana, marveled at the production of Asasia cloth, the original Kente, woven in narrow strips with intricate patterns specially created for the king. Little did the Dane know that narrow strip weaving had been produced in Africa since the 11th century.

Art is loved and appreciated in Africa not only for its visual riches but also for the social and religious roles it plays for the living, and sometimes the dead. Figures carved in a Cameroonian stool can preserve a mythic story for generations; motifs on a Nupe door can evoke spirits to protect one from harm or evil forces; and figures created by the Hemba of Zaire represent ancestors, creating bonds with those who have passed on. Some figures ensure healthy offspring or bridge communication with an unborn child; during the course of the day a figurine can be prayed to, washed, fed, or worn for adornment.

"In Africa, art is for life's sake," says Dr. Kariamu Welsh-Asante, a professor of African-American Studies at Temple University in Philadelphia and one of the homeowners featured in these pages. "Traditionally, if art did not contribute to the good of the community, it wasn't made." It

north africa

is small wonder that African art objects, highly respected by their own makers, have also become sought-after treasures in the rest of the world. And these artistic expressions provide ample opportunity to add beauty and ease to our lives through the form of interior decoration.

African inspiration in the West's fine and decorative arts has come in three major waves. The first came with the spread of Egyptian art and design during the Napoleonic period at the start of the 1800s. It was expressed first in the creation of furniture—some initially commissioned by Napoleon—followed by architecture and fashion. For instance, leg supports with carved bulls and lions, simple stools with rush seats, as well as lotus and papyrus patterns were beautifully reincarnated as Egyptian Revival furnishings. The second wave lasted from about 1905 into the early 1930s, and influenced art, music, literature, history, and furnishings during the Jazz Age, particularly in Paris. And today, we are experiencing a third wave in contemporary art, fashion, furnishings, film, literature, and music.

Taking a closer look at the second wave reveals the impact of Africa on the European art community of the early 1900s. This community was made up of an active circle of friends and associates always on the lookout for unique approaches to enrich their work. Members of the group, including Braque, Derain, Vlaminck, Picasso, and Matisse, would meet in museums, bistros, and studios to share ideas, criticism, praise, and new trends. According to his autobiography, one day when Maurice Vlaminck was in need of extra money, he sold his masks from Benin (previously Dahomey) and the Ivory Coast to André Derain. Picasso and Matisse saw the masks for the first time during a visit to Derain's home in 1905, and were awestruck by their creativity. No fans of representational art, the painters found the freedom of expression in the masks liberating.

Needless to say, this exposure greatly influenced their work. In fact, Picasso's works of 1907 and 1908 are characterized as the Période Négre because of the parallels between his simple abstract forms and those found in African art; the influence of Egyptian paintings and Congolese carved masks is especially striking in his painting *Les Demoiselles d'Avignon*. Matisse was also captivated by African art and his sculptures from 1908 reflect his love of the progressive simplicity of African form. "Modern art would not be what it is today if the European artist had not come into contact with African art and borrowed many of its images and concepts," stresses Warren Robbins, founding director emeritus and senior scholar at the National Museum of African Art in Washington, D.C.

The taste for African and African-influenced art swept through Europe during the early years of the century. While Germany was experiencing similar influences as France, the allure of Africa was perhaps most pronounced in Paris. Archaeological discoveries, especially the opening of Tutankhamen's tomb in Egypt, captured a great deal of attention. Josephine Baker was dancing her way into French hearts and minds; expatriate authors from Harlem, such as James Baldwin, Countee Cullen, Langston Hughes, and Richard Wright, were exploding onto the literary scene; and jazz and blues musicians had sophisticates tapping their toes to a new beat. And what Picasso did with his paintings, Pierre Legrain did with his furniture designs (see page 92). Both masters achieved new looks characterized by Africa's distinguished past.

THE LOOK AND FEEL OF AFRICA

African art is a feast for the eyes. It is the vibrant, colorful beauty of fabric worn by women in a Senegalese marketplace, each print different and each more beautiful than the next. It is the vitality of African-inspired interiors: bold primaries, deep earth tones, subtle neutrals, and gentle pastels are equally at home with this style. Textures are also important to African style, from silk and cotton to wood, raffia, bark, mud, or shells. Whether it's silky soft Ewe cloth from Ghana or the discreet, subtle warmth of sisal, Africa offers a wealth of textural options.

African style has many faces, just like any other design profile. It can be traditional, classical, contemporary, bohemian, minimal, trendy, or quirky. It can also follow regional traditions that produce more distinct interpretations. Authenticity in these specific styles requires some knowledge of how African art and design evolved in different parts of the continent. Each region has its own unique set of visual cues, and the thoughtful use of these motifs can create a well-defined design.

WEST AFRICA: This region offers the most familiar and popular of all the design expressions exported from Africa. It is characterized by pulsating colors, bold patterns, fluid forms, and simple geometry. Its design characteristics are casual, rather than orchestrated: you use what you have. Since some of the world's most exquisite sculpture is produced in West and Central Africa, wood-carved masks and figures are the essence of this expression. Facial masks, helmet masks, and ceremonial dance masks—some as tall as 6 feet—are all very important.

The choice of furnishings includes wood, leather, wrought iron, or other pieces with natural finishes. Consider Asante stools, Nigerian chairs, and regional basketry, pottery, and other functional art. Handwoven Kente cloths, Adinkra prints, Ewe cloth made of silk, indigo resist-dyed Adire cloth, or mud cloths from Mali are at home in a West African ambience as wall hangings, pillowcases and covers, or as throws for the sofas and chairs. Painted wall surfaces mirror body decoration or decorative murals painted by the women of West and sub-Saharan Africa.

EAST AFRICA:
When evoking this region, the emphasis rests on the coexistence of people, land, and wildlife. While East Africa is a blending of many ethnic groups, the Masai seem to best embody the spirit of this part of the continent and its style. East African expression is simple but distinctive, reflecting a sense of adventure and a straightforward approach to life. This style has a freer quality, one which mirrors the Masai's nomadic life of cattle herding.

The focus here is on texture, color, and light. The color palette includes muted earth tones, taken from the terrain of the east and the savannah grasslands. The feel is dry: dusty beiges, rusts, browns, yellows, oranges, and ochers dominate, with an introduction of red plaids and stripes. Furniture made of rattan, rush, twig, wicker, leather, and straw fits the mood, while the rugged textures of sisal, jute, and sea grass continue the organic feel of this look. Pine, ash, beech, cedar, and other woods add a clean, light ambience. Walls are cream, beige, or rust, and using glazes to add texture is a wonderful touch: an ocher glaze or wash, for example, adds an honest, organic feel to any space. Masai spears and walking sticks, Ethiopian chairs and stools, or colorful Turkanar beadwork all find a place here. East Africa offers not a sumptuous style, but rather a sense of timeless, natural integrity.

NORTH AFRICA:
Morocco, Tunisia, and Algeria are rich in intricate art, ceramics, tiles, rugs, and carpets. Traditionally, the people of this region were nomadic camel herders. They crisscrossed the desert in merchant caravans, trading with the peoples of the sub-Sahara as well as with Islamic peoples to the east. The look from this region is a mixture of vivid colors and brilliant patterns; stucco, slate, stone, wrought iron, and adobe architecture all reflect a land of camel caravans, bustling outdoor marketplaces, and desert oases where color and texture are overlapping and electric.

The North African look is a layered one, with deeply colored, geometrically patterned wool rugs of all sizes used for floors or walls; ceramic tiles covering floors, walls, and stairs; and vibrant textile strips joined to cover pillows and cushions or used to drape over furniture. Simple upholstered pieces are common here, with lots of pillows for lounging. No references to people and animals are made in the decorative patterns because of the Muslim prohibition against representational art; the emphasis is instead on dynamic geometric motifs.

CLASSIC AFRO-EURO:
The style that results from the influence of African motifs on European designs is often full of elegance, comfort, quality, and grandeur. This style incorporates traditional European furniture design and architecture, layered with formal African design and artistic craftsmanship. The effects are striking.

Colors here are deep and rich. Furniture is dark and tropical, featuring mahogany, African oak, and ebony, and the standards of craftsmanship are exquisite. The furnishings are usually classically European while upholsteries, walls, floors, and rugs are African or African inspired.

This means that a French Empire sofa might be upholstered in handwoven African fabrics with gold threading, geometrics, or animal patterns, all calling into play symbols associated with the continent. Add to this a strikingly bold, colorful backdrop of freehand painting, with deep washes and glazes, and a geometric parquet floor, and the stage is set for decorative drama.

MODERN: The emphasis in this African-inspired style is on design; comfort is a close second. The look is sophisticated and stylishly modern: the elements are warm, but the style is cool. The African art used in this interpretation is applied discreetly. The ideal choice of sculpture for this style would be pieces that are minimal or abstract in design, such as Fang or Kota sculpture from Gabon or figurines from Burkina Faso. Zairian Kuba cloth and Showa textiles are ideal, since their monochromatic color schemes and angular style of repetitive geometrics are both simple and sophisticated. Furniture displays clean lines and simple angular or curvilinear forms.

This look offers great design flexibility. You can mix furniture from different periods and parts of the world as long as the pieces have a contemporary feeling. White walls in any shade work well, but so do blues and grays. Natural wood floors in light shades of ash, beech, birch, or pine provide a warm organic feeling, as do natural floor coverings such as sisal carpet, sea grass, or low-pile wools.

Wherever it originates, African style requires several things of us: imagination, resourcefulness, clever design solutions, inventive ways of reinterpreting the traditional, and a willingness to use our hands in the spirit of the African artisans. Regardless of your particular preferences, consider producing your own work, whether it is recycling a sofa, reupholstering furniture with an Ashoke textile, or painting a freehand window trim. As Africans have long known, we can all become artists, telling our stories through the objects and spaces we create.

afro-euro

If first impressions are in fact lasting, then it is the entrance of your home that will communicate what you and your family are all about. This is by far the most utilitarian area of the home, where we make the daily transition from outside activities to the private world of family. However, the entrance should be more than a storage space for coats and umbrellas; it is the place where we welcome our friends and family to share our home. Around the continent of Africa, entrance architec-

entrances and halls

ture and greeting rituals may vary, yet many design features found there, both in the past and present, can be attractively transplanted anywhere. Whether your home is large or small, these elements can exert a strong presence in your entrance in functional and decorative ways. For example, guests make a grand entrance to artist Helen Bershad's town house in the Center City area of Philadelphia, where a 20-foot-long handwoven Kuba ceremonial skirt from Zaire runs the entire length of the entry

hall. Coauthor Sharne Algotsson and her husband, Jan, also live in Philadelphia, but their entrance is smaller and more intimate. The Algotssons have taken full advantage of their stairs, walls, and floor space to paint motifs, hang textiles, and place runners and mats here and there, creating a lively welcome.

As transitional spaces, entrances and halls can offer room for extra display or storage. You may find the perfect spot in your entrance for a table that doesn't quite fit elsewhere or for shelves in search of a wall. When space is at a premium, start with the floor and work your way up, using wall surfaces to introduce decorative elements that do not require lots of room. This includes masks, textiles, basketry, paintings, mirrors with decorative frames, works of art, jewelry, and hats. A mirror is always an excellent addition to an entrance for functional reasons, but it also gives the illusion of making your space seem larger. And when placed opposite a window, the mirror can reflect light to make your hall brighter.

FROM THE BOTTOM UP

Consider how best to use the floor space of your entrance. If heavy traffic is a concern, choose low-pile, easy-to-clean rugs, carpets, and rimmers or runners. Floor coverings with patterns are an excellent choice: they do not show dirt and soil as easily as solid-colored rugs. It is also a good idea to use stationary rug pads under throws, area rugs, and mats to keep them safely in place.

Organic fibers like sisal, jute, sea grass, wool, cotton, and other natural materials bring a warm, natural feel to floor coverings for an African look. Coauthor Denys Davis, for example, layered several lightweight Moroccan area rugs to give the entrance to her Philadelphia home a North African ambience. On the other hand, Drs. Molefe and Kariamu Welsh-Asante created a more formal center hall entrance. They covered their floor with a radiant handwoven Kuba-inspired carpet designed by James Tufenkian and paired it with a circular table of inlaid mahogany, zebrawood, and African walnut. The Davis and Welsh-Asante entrances are both very African, yet offer two distinctly different interpretations.

If you would love color and pattern for your entrance floor, yet are concerned about traffic flow, cleaning, or other kinds of maintenance, consider freehand painting and stenciling. These are wonderful solutions for incorporating African designs and motifs into your space, bringing the tradition of decorative painting to your home. Your per-

PRECEDING PAGE: A 20-foot-long piece of Kuba cloth from Zaire graces this long, narrow hallway, serving as the equivalent of an African-style red carpet for guests who enter painter Helen Bershad's home in the Center City area of Philadelphia. Spotlights overhead highlight the cloth's rich texture and striking lines.

OPPOSITE: Sculptor, painter, and designer Armand P. Arman and his wife, Corice, have placed a Gaudi settee and mirror in the entrance hall of their New York home side by side with an elongated mask from Burkina Faso. An anthropomorphic Lobi stool nestles uder the settee, while a mirror reflects part of the Armans' extensive collection of masks.

OVERLEAF, LEFT: An assortment of shapes and angles is strikingly displayed against a neutral background in the entrance to textile dealer Veronica Robertson's loft in Manhattan; *Totem of the World*, a sculpture by Tyrone Mitchell, contrasts colorfully with the Tji Wara mask by the Bambara of Mali.

OVERLEAF, RIGHT: A wrought-iron console table recalling the craftsmanship of African blacksmiths holds family photos, flowers, and other items that add a welcoming feeling near the entrance of Richard and Jeanne Presha's home. Above are prints, a mask embellished with cowrie shells, a portrait by an unknown painter, and an old map of Africa.

sonal version can evoke a North African floral mosaic tile design or feature a single Ghanaian Adinkra symbol. These visual delights will add character to your room and give even the smallest space a feeling of drama. Whatever decorating decisions you make, keep in mind that entrances are intimately connected with adjacent rooms. The design should flow from one space to the next, without jarring your aesthetic sense.

Treated wall surfaces can do more to create a specific mood for

ABOVE: These exquisite Bakota figures from Gabon were used to guard the personal belongings of the dead.

RIGHT: From the first step into this center hall, it is clear that well-traveled collectors reside here: Owners Drs. Molefe and Kariamu Welsh-Asante are in fact the driving force behind the philosophy of Afrocentricity and have made many visits to the continent. In their entrance, the tradition of fine wood inlay is re-created in the application of geometric shapes in such tropical woods as mahogany, zebrawood, and African walnut, designed by Giovanni Massaglia. James Tufenkian designed the handwoven carpet, dubbed "Kente," and inspired by West African weaving traditions.

RIGHT: Denys Davis transformed an awkward space beneath her entrance staircase into a cozy reading area. She reupholstered a Victorian settee in a machine-made Kente cloth and added contrasting pillows, one dotted with cowrie shells. Davis lined the edge of the mantelpiece with an African motif and filled the area with a hodge-podge of other items from the continent, including an African stool that doubles as a table, a drum, a basket woven from telephone wire, and diverse carvings.

OPPOSITE: While short on space, this simple entrance takes advantage of the walls and floors to make a statement in Sharne Algotsson's Philadelphia home. The varying shades of the monochromatic palette highlight the richness of the Showa and Kasai woven mats; these velvet and cut-pile raffia mats were once considered extremely valuable and were used as a form of currency. The beech floor, sisal runner, and wool carpet radiate the warmth of natural materials; the curves of the Thonet chair and twig stool echo the lines of the Kenyan walking sticks; and the Dogon mask and the portrait of an African prince, by painter Sam Finch, help evoke the spirit of African style.

your entrance or hall than any other element. The West African–inspired staircase and corridor design painted by Santino Croci in Stephan Janson's home on page 46 is a wonderful tribute to the women of Nigeria. While this mural design may be too ambitious a project for some homes, consider a smaller, simpler pattern, a ceiling trim, or a continuous stenciled pattern that runs around door and window frames. Be aware that large patterns usually require a large wall and, conversely, patterns that are tiny may lack impact. And if you wish to achieve subtle drama, consider distressed or broken color. This will give a warm, textured feeling to your walls and at the same time disguise any imperfections.

THE ARTISTRY OF DOORS

Doors are an often overlooked architectural feature that can nonetheless bring a life of their own to any space. Consider the island of Lamu off the coast of Kenya, which is known for its exterior doors. Streets are so narrow there that more attention was paid to the doors than to

OPPOSITE: **Bright trompe l'oeil tiles framing the entrance to the Davises' Victorian home give their sun porch the look and feel of Morocco; the design and colors on this archway were inspired by the tiles that are ubiquitous in North Africa.**

THIS PAGE, TOP: **A quilt entitled "Women's Work" by Lucille Clark of Philadelphia adds warmth to a hall in artist Barbara Carter's house in Brooklyn. Wooden floors, plants, and artifacts recall the African emphasis on natural materials. A detail of Clark's quilt demonstrates that a woman's work is never done: the two women depicted combine their maternal**

and culinary roles, crushing grain for future meals with their swaddled babies secure against their backs. The panel is also representative of the African textile tradition of appliqué.

the facade of the stone houses in town. This has contributed to a wealth of elaborately carved doors, found even on some mud and thatched houses. Koranic messages, organic symbols, or geometric shapes are carved into the wood. The ornate designs usually adorn the frame, lintel, and center post, and carvers responsible for them are held in high regard.

Meanwhile in Libya, the entrances to the whitewashed houses in the Old City of Tripoli are framed by stone doorways, providing a stark contrast to the plain houses. Elaborate carvings typically present motifs based on foliage or flowers; sometimes the designs cover everything from the overhead panels to the doorjambs. In other parts of Libya there are doors made of palm planks that are painted with intricate designs.

In Morocco, doors may have a Fatima head hanging nearby to ward off evil spirits. These wooden doors are often painted with intriguing Islamic-influenced geometrics and mosaic patterns in striking primaries and pastels. Some entrances feature doors within doors that provide protection from intruders, as well as privacy. The Dagara people in Burkina Faso also ward off evil spirits by hiding a specific juju, or charm, near the entrance by which spiritual ancestors provide protection. But their climate is so warm that houses have no doors, symbolic of the community's open arms.

Since so many homes in Africa are part of family compounds with common entrances and meeting areas, they tend to have a strong communal orientation that is welcoming by nature. For example, the Nyakyusa people of Tanzania spend a great deal of time around the family campfires. Common meeting areas are also part of the Ndebele areas of South Africa, where, against the colorful backdrop on a painted exterior house wall, men in the community gather or family members and guests assemble for ceremonies. A lower wall flanking

RIGHT: This hall rack, with its Ghanaian straw hat, captures the organic simplicity of African forms. OPPOSITE: Angular patterns borrowed from the Ndebele people of South Africa complement the low arched window in the Davises' landing, and the bold shades of red-orange, leaf green, and slate blue add interest to an otherwise starkly white area. The landing is large enough to accommodate the flow of traffic up and down the stairs as well as a small chair that serves as a resting spot for an African basket.

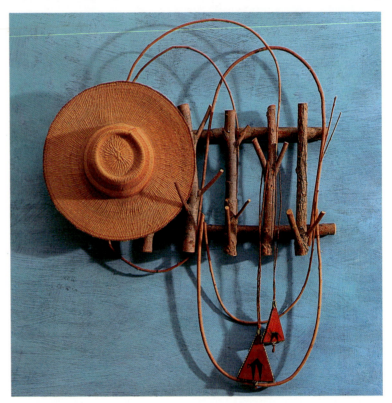

the gateway can offer built-in seating or a platform when necessary, and the designs on the main wall surrounding the entrance are nothing short of mesmerizing.

While the physical treatment of entrances may differ from culture to culture, their meaning and significance are fairly universal. As the passageway from the outer world, this place of welcome offers pleasant anticipation of what lies beyond. A warm and inviting entrance conveys the same meaning as the Yoruba greeting "e k'abo," which means "glad to meet you," or "glad to see you're back!"

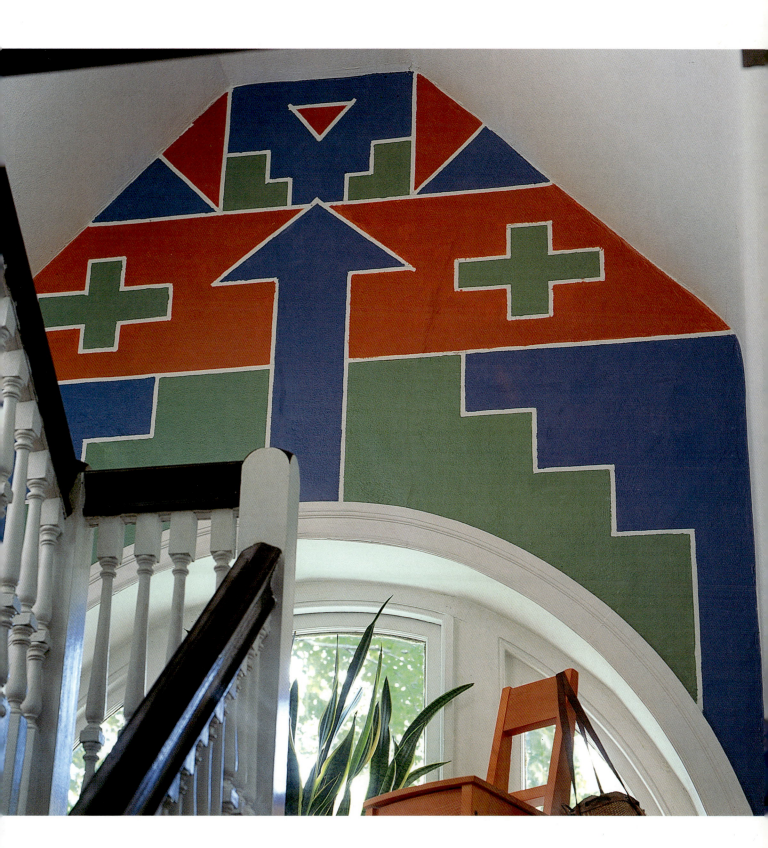

Consider the vivid beauty of bougainvillea as it paints a magenta portrait along a dusty roadside, or the maze of strong lines traveling along a piece of Kuba cloth, or the golden, silky smoothness of amber beads. The visual and tactile elements of color, pattern, and texture bring gratification to our experience of the natural and man-made world. They compel us to look, touch, and wonder; they evoke associations; and they can quite literally create moods as we absorb their sensual messages.

COLOR, PATTERN, TEXTURE

Every physical thing that we encounter is characterized by color, conveying emotion, power, presence, and sensibility. Color can conjure up feelings of happiness, tranquility, sadness, anxiety, excitement. It is an unspoken communicator capable of singular and very direct messages: uniforms in blue, gray, or black deliver a different message than do those in white, red, or pink. People of different societies and cultures have distinctive perceptions of color, often with conflicting meanings. And once

those color associations are established, it is difficult to disassociate them.

There is no way to think of Africa or its art and design without considering the impact of color. From Egypt to South Africa, color is the common denominator; it is everywhere and in everything. It is the quintessential element in the natural world, and where it does not exist, Africans have inserted it in imaginative combinations, as in the indigo Adire cloths created by the Yoruba people of Nigeria; the strong reds, yellows, greens, and blacks of Kente cloth from the Asante of Ghana; the colorful beaded corsets worn by the Dinka of East Africa; the deep, saturated hues of Moroccan rugs; or the golden luster of massive earrings worn by the Fulani of the western Sudan.

The array of colors that characterize African clothing is often produced from natural pigments. When it comes to dyeing wools, cottons, raffia, and the fibers used for basketry, indigo is the most widely used organic dye of them all. In Egypt, indigo dyeing predates the time of Christ, but its ancient cultural roots reach throughout the continent. For instance, dyers in the Hausa city of Kano,

Nigeria, have produced a wide variety of remarkable indigo cloths, including some with a metallic sheen, while the Yoruba have perfected the art of indigo resist-dyeing in the form of Adire cloth.

Producing indigo dye is a lengthy and complicated process. The dye is obtained from plants of the genus Indigofera, which contain a sugar and indigo compound that triggers a fermentation process. First the leaves are crushed, pounded, and molded into balls. The balls sit for several days to allow the fermentation to take place. The second stage also requires several days. During this time, dry wood is placed in a kiln to produce ash. The ash is then molded into balls with the rich blue water of the fermented leaves. The saturated balls are broken and placed on a sieve of twigs sandwiched between a pair of stacked kilns. Water is poured into the top kiln, where it is filtered through the sieve to form a pool of dye. The number of ash balls determines the intensity of the dye, from the palest of hues to the blackest blue. Imagine the impact that a variety of deeply saturated indigo elements can bring to a room!

There are several points to consider when bringing the feeling of Africa into your house through the use of color. First and foremost, experiment with colors that feel at home in your life. If, for example, you are comfortable with pastels, don't try to incorporate the bold colors of Ghanaian Kente cloth. Think instead of the sensations and images that you would like to surround yourself with, and find colors that suggest these associations.

In the Algotssons' living room, for example, the colors were all taken

RIGHT: Extra seating in the Algotssons' morning room is provided by this wisdom knot stool from Ghana.

OPPOSITE: A friend of the Algotssons' dubbed their small morning room "Mood Indigo." It gains its strength from the color and pattern that have been applied everywhere: the gold leaf and painted indigo walls, the shimmery diamond-patterned sofa upholstery, and the Nigerian strip-weave textile with gold Lurex and metallic threads. An Asante stool, a Fang mask from Gabon on the wall, a Dogon mask from Mali on the table, and a sequined Haitian prayer cloth add more layers.

OVERLEAF: As a self-professed global citizen, designer Stephan Janson makes his home amid the exotic. The walls of his Milan showroom are painted to replicate Nigerian women's frescoes; the mural was painted by Santino Croci.

from the savannah grasslands of East Africa. The ocher walls create a golden tone that becomes almost liquid as the light pours in. The room also emanates a rustic and rugged tone that is consistent with the imagery of this pastoral cattle-herding region. The fabrics and furnishings were selected for their kinship with the colors of the Kenyan landscape and to reflect the Masai and Turkanar love of reds. It is all African, as you'll discover if you close your eyes and think of East Africa. The vision will be different, but the colors will be the same.

A PANORAMA OF PATTERNS

There was a time when squiggly, zigzag configurations and lots of dots were used as the stereotypical African patterns. You've probably seen these easily recognized graphics in commercial packaging, and the connection is instantaneous. However, visual clichés are today being upstaged by a multitude of authentic design styles. This is a result

of such factors as a growing understanding of African art and design, increased interaction with Africans from all parts of the continent, the popularity of Africa as a travel destination, and notable exposure in the media. Design traditions from diverse ethnic groups are showcased in books such as *The African Mural* by Paul Changuion, *African Canvas* by Margaret Courtney-Clark, *Morocco* by Dennis and Lisl Landt, and *Africa Adorned* by Angela Fisher. In such works, the art of Africa is not taken out of context, but presented as an integral part of day-to-day life.

One message delivered in all of these books is the strong attachment Africans have for the art of patterns. It is an appreciation nurtured at a very young age, so that one grows up with an eye for

OPPOSITE: This popular contemporary Moroccan pattern is widely used on ceramics and pottery. Such vibrant hues and pulsating patterns abound in the northern regions of Africa.

THIS PAGE, LEFT: A Liberian chief's chair rests on a tile made of African slate.

RIGHT: A kaleidoscope of patterns is created by the Moroccan tiles, bowls, and stone floor in Carlos Ascher's dining room at his Philadelphia town house.

ABOVE: The colors and objects of this still life convey the warmth of equatorial Africa to a kitchen wall of the Manhattan apartment of Robert Teszar, a stylist and set decorator. His collection of every-day objects and tropical fruit evokes the simple life, where hands still produce the necessities of life. OPPOSITE: An assemblage of table-ware patterns complements these place mats made of such natural elements as root, twine twig, bamboo, wood bead, and straw. The hand-painted tiles offer another approach to incorporating pattern into the tabletop.

aesthetics and an ability to see beauty in almost anything. The Kuba children of Zaire, for example, begin drawing and experimenting with patterns in the soil when they are tiny; some of them grow up to create remarkable textiles that are admired throughout the world for the complexity of their patterns. One account that reveals the Kuba people's appreciation for patterns is the story of a king who was given the present of a motorcycle in the 1920s. It was not the motorcycle itself that gave him the most pleasure, however, but the patterns that he was able to make with the tires in the dirt: these were new designs that he had never before seen.

The richness of African patterns is truly astonishing. It is an art fueled by the land's wonderful endowment of resources and materials, a love of natural forms, cultural ideologies rich with symbolism, and the creative resourcefulness that ingeniously ties all these elements together to create complex patterns. These come into play everywhere. Just think of the panorama of patterns found on stools, doors, buildings, gold weights, textiles, staffs, gourds, basketry, and even on bodies in the form of painting and scarification techniques. While some symbols and motifs are decorative, most are symbolic, full of ritual meaning. Some are contemporary, and others are centuries old. They issue warnings and extend welcomes. What unites them is that they are all original and rife with an asymmetrical rhythm and vitality, partners in the dance of design.

Pattern styles are strongly determined by an artist's religious affiliation and by the traditions of his or her ethnic group. The Kuba of Zaire, for instance, favor motifs that are angular and repetitive. In the design of their masks, the Bwa and Mossi of Burkina Faso prefer checkerboards and triangular designs in dark and light tones, symbolizing good and evil, night and day, male and female. In Ghana, the luxurious cloths worn by Akan chiefs are embroidered with such symbols of leadership as the double crocodile with one stomach, which expresses the need to share, or the shield flanked by birds, symbolizing the Ghanaian national government. And there are traditions within traditions. An Ndebele woman may uphold the time-honored practice

of painting the outside of her home in geometric patterns; these result in the explosion of color found in South Africa's countryside. But the pattern that a woman uses is uniquely hers: people know her style as well as they know her name, and the pattern will also be found in her beadwork and on the interior walls of her home.

At the other end of this spectrum of pattern are those creative designs that are amalgams of multiple influences, exotic products of merging cultures and art traditions. Unlike Zaire, for example, which has a very homogeneous design tradition with almost no outside influences, Morocco could be characterized as a treasure trove of design brimming with color, pattern, and texture, revealing the country's fusion of North African, Berber, Islamic, European, and Sudanese influences. This mixture yields the vivacious and even whimsical design combinations found in adobe architecture as well as the gloriously colored tiled and painted floors, murals and frescoes, pottery, metalwork, fabrics, jewelry, and more: patterns and motifs vie for attention in

LEFT: Denys Davis gave this old chair a new lease on life with a bit of paint, some Kuba cloth, and a raffia skirt. Now known as "Kuba Dancer," this chair has so much spirit and verve that it is hard to get someone to sit still in it.
OPPOSITE: The frescoes of Stephan Janson's stairwell reflect the joyous spontaneity of the West African mural.

the most dynamic fashion. Islam, which forbids the depiction of human or animal forms in art, could be seen as a hindrance to the creative process. But it served in fact as a challenger to creativity, an invitation to elaborate on patterns of all kinds, including florals, mosaics, geometrics, stripes, and such symbols as the crescent and star, or the hand of Fatima, which protects against the evil eye. Some patterns are so detailed, in fact, that they seem textural.

Adinkra patterns designed by the Asante of Ghana date back to the early 1800s. They comprise a series of symbols that are used to adorn the traditional mourning cloth. Legend has it that the name Adinkra comes from the name Adintera, which means farewell or good-bye; hence the use of Adinkra for funerals. There are at least a hundred known symbols used in Adinkra cloth, imprinted by carved stamps made from pieces of calabash, a hard-shelled fruit. The dye used in this application is a thick, tarlike solution made from tree bark boiled with lumps of iron slag. When the cloth is completely stamped, it will be made up of squares filled with one symbol repeated thirty to forty times on cotton fabric, in red, blue-green, brown, or purple.

Each square will have a meaning, and the total design offers a beautiful expression of vernacular imagery. For example, a heart-shaped pattern with coiled ends is called "Sankofa," which means "to return and fetch it." Another common shape is the fern, or "Aya," a symbol of defiance, while the moon represents love and kindness. In the West, these traditional designs have surfaced in the work of modern artists, from Henri Matisse to Keith Haring.

A TOUCH OF TEXTURE

Unlike color and pattern, texture is experienced not only through the eyes but also through the skin. It creates a sensation—or the illusion of one—through the quality of an object's surface. The illusion of density or weight, for example, can be achieved through the use of deep-set texture. Similarly, shiny and matte surfaces that are the same color and tone can appear to be darker or lighter. Other effects can be achieved by changing the direction of the pattern grain.

OPPOSITE: Keith Haring was one of the many celebrated artists who successfully incorporated elements of African art and design into their work. Here, one of his prints forms the backdrop for an eclectic assortment of treasured objects, including an example of the black memorabilia that is highly sought after by collectors of all backgrounds.

RIGHT: Vegetables in a woven raffia basket from Kenya, a twig placemat from the Philippines, and tiles hand-painted in warm colors with organic patterns create a rich scheme of color, pattern, and texture in honor of nature's bounty. OPPOSITE: This close-up of Willem and Margreet Monster's tabletop is a feast for the eyes: the bold and colorful modern tableware patterns, manufactured by Swid Powell, work well with an authentic Pakhamani tablecloth from South Africa as well as with the rich hues of the fruit.

Texture and tactility are inherently sensual qualities, and Africa is a continent where people have retained close ties to the sensual world. It is a land where textiles, buildings, tools, utensils, jewelry, instruments, and so many other objects are made by hand, using natural materials. And the basic building blocks of African creativity are literally earthbound: mud, twigs, wood, straw, bark, sand, stone, pebbles, clay, and so on. Things made with these ingredients take on an even richer personality when exposed to wind, rain, and sun.

Texture's illusive qualities are important in replicating the feel of Africa in interior design. Surfaces that are coarse, knotty, uneven, fibrous, or grainy are experienced as being rustic and primal, while light, sheer, smooth surfaces are interpreted as being soft, refined, and elegant. The dynamics of texture are even more powerful when combined: the feeling of soft and hard, light and heavy, or synthetic and natural can produce unexpected but exciting results. Mixing textures like this can also create a level of detail in interiors that compounds their interest and enhances the overall impression.

COLOR, PATTERN, TEXTURE

Don't be afraid to combine a variety of textures. Follow the rules, or break them all to make up your own. You'll find that wicker, twig, stone, wrought iron, terra-cotta, cottons, sisal, and sea grass can provide a light, airy feel, while mahogany and other hard woods, satin, damasks, brass, marble, and slate feel weightier. Be subtle or obvious, but go for a few surprises!

**In** America, family rooms, entertainment centers, dens, and even kitchens are upstaging living rooms as the center of family activity. But a living room should still be a favorite room in the home for gathering together your family and guests. A place of contrasts, it should feel so comfortable that people are lured back again and again, with a strong urge perhaps to curl up on the sofa. At the

living rooms

same time, a living room should feel special enough to be the centerpiece of a home. It takes time, however, for a beautiful room to develop. New furniture, no matter how wonderful, does not automatically create a wonderful living space. Rather, you decorate from life experiences, using pieces with meaning, history, and beauty.

As one of the most public rooms of a home, the living room showcases your finest possessions. It is a prime spot to display treasures of the past, favorite family mementos, and wonderful finds from near and far. Every living room featured here shares an

appreciation for African style. These rooms are excellent examples of how you can interweave African and African-influenced pieces to create a very personal collage, both functional and decorative. In Carlos Ascher's town house in Philadelphia, for instance, Moroccan rugs and vibrantly patterned leather ottomans function as sources of warmth and comfort. Armand and Corice Arman enjoy their museum-quality collection of nail-studded fetish symbols, which stand guard in their living room. And Cheryl Riley, a furniture designer in San Francisco, has created a series of creative "Zulu Tables" for her living room, linking the geometric shape of the letter **Z** with the energy of the Zulu people.

THE MIX: MAKING IT WORK

Tying different elements together is the spirit of African style. Imaginative interpretations are found in all interior decoration, but this inspirational mix is especially important in African expressions. It is in keeping with the resourcefulness of Africans, who often work within limitations, making something from nothing or creatively enhancing an existing environment.

Most interior decorating styles start with furniture, choosing

PRECEDING PAGE: Wood and iron Masai spears intersect on the wall above a sofa in the Algotssons' living room, transporting family and friends to East Africa. The symmetrical architectural details add an air of formality, while the Ethiopian chair, Senufo stool, and tiny Masai stool give a rustic elegance. The red throw and pillows are reminiscent of the Masai, and the interplay of textures—cotton, wool, parchment, wicker, twig, sisal, wood, and metal—contributes to the organic feeling created by the dusty, muted earth tones of the sofa, area rug, and textiles.

LEFT: Sharne Algotsson turned to a combination of West African patterns for inspiration in painting the trim around her family's bay windows. She used a combing technique along with freehand drawings to vary the textures of the two layers of paint.

OPPOSITE: Paint and pattern are effective and inexpensive ways to bring the influence of African art into your home. The color and texture of ocher-glazed walls enhance the warmth of the Algotssons' living room. Seat cushions on the sofa are covered with a commercial reproduction of Korhogo cloth, which was originally used for hunters' garments. A corner contains a wooden table topped with a calabash gourd, clay pots, and guitar covered with cowrie shells. Below the table is a Moroccan shopping basket.

ABOVE: This sofa is a study in contrasts by Alex Locadia, featuring a smooth leather surface with scarification patterns, a carved wooden section, and a hornlike leg that has been turned on a lathe.

RIGHT: Locadia's creative use of textures is evidenced by his sleekly smooth totem and black leather chair, set off against a black geometric table with gouges in all the right places.

OPPOSITE: A small Brooklyn studio overflows with original pieces, including art furniture and totemic structures by Locadia. Zebra and leopard prints along with an assortment of figurines grace the "Aboriginal" couch. The kitchen houses the "Mahalia" chair that sits in front of the "Plop" lamp. Locadia, a highly regarded artist and furniture designer, is known for fusing traditional African techniques with high technology, as if searching for design cues from various centuries aboard one of the Jetsons' spaceships.

among a wide variety of sofas, chairs, and tables and then basing the room around these choices. But because of cultural preferences, functional needs, and religious beliefs, African furniture has traditionally revolved around stools and mats, particularly in sub-Saharan areas. This has meant a greater stylistic role for African textiles, sculptures, masks, and other objects. Thus it is often the use of fabrics and patterns that serves as a decorative starting point, with the furniture selection following. For example, you can create a strong visual impact in your living room by choosing Asoke, a durable handwoven textile with metallic threads made by the Yoruba in Nigeria, and then finding a sofa style that could serve as a compatible base for this upholstery.

Similarly, art and sculpture can serve as a decorative springboard. One of the characteristics of this art is how evocative it is. Its range of imagery is astonishingly diverse, with colors and forms borrowed from nature, then transformed to create striking geometrics and unique sculptural lines. All of this can be a rich source of inspiration, calling for a bit of imagination and resourcefulness.

In the living room, as elsewhere in the home, color, texture, form, and proportion are at their best when in balance. This can be accom-

plished, for example, by pairing the bold graphics of Korhogo textiles, designed by the Senufo of the Ivory Coast, with the smaller, repetitive patterns of Adinkra prints from Ghana, or by placing an Ethiopian ladderback chair near a brushed aluminum table with a frosted glass top. At first glance, these elements may seem to have nothing in common. But together, they share uncomplicated, simple form—one of the hallmarks of modernity—as well as a pleasingly textured quality.

In designing a living room, it is of course possible to focus on the individual look of a specific region in Africa—say, the northwestern coastal area or the eastern part of the continent. One excellent example of this selectivity is the home of Carlos Ascher in Philadelphia, whose interiors are unforgettably Moroccan. His collection of layered Moroccan carpets and rugs revels in strong, almost electric, primary colors. Intricately patterned pillows and ottomans are then combined and placed with the casual off-hand confidence that comes naturally to the homes of Morocco.

Another example is the living room of Roger Prigent in Manhattan. His classic Egyptian Revival and Empire decor expresses the look of traditional Euro-Egyptian design. Incorporating such symbolic elements as sphinxes, scarabs, and pyramids, his living room show-

OPPOSITE: From the top floor of a former pickle factory in Manhattan, Armand P. Arman, his wife, Corice, and their two children take in a sweeping view of the Hudson River. Prolific assemblages of fine art, tools, violins, radios, coffee grinders, loom pulleys, and reliquary figures from Gabon make up what artist Arman calls their "accumulations." In the living room, open shelving and bookcases provide homes for an ever-expanding collection of masks and carved wooden figures. The sofa and chairs were designed by Le Corbusier in 1928 and the wooden stool is from North Africa. Hanging on the wall are two Andy Warhol portraits of Corice Arman.
ABOVE: This painting from Frank Stella's "Concentric" series serves as a good balance for the Armans' collection of Congolese power figures or *nkisi*, which are studded with nails and blades. Traditionally, these fetishes were used for protection, healing, oath taking, or to indicate the guilt or innocence of a person on trial.

living rooms

OPPOSITE: Roger Prigent, a former French fashion photographer and now a collector and owner of Malmaison Antiques in New York City, conveys the drama of Egyptian design through his lavish approach to decoration, with early Empire furnishings capturing the opulence of this look. In Prigent's

living room, white brick walls with exposed beams and an Islamic-styled geometric-patterned floor harmonize with gold-leaf furniture, a Senufo chair, leopard patterns, and West African sculpture. ABOVE: Prigent carries African imagery down to the smallest detail with this gold-leaf finial in the form of a spearhead.

THIS PAGE, TOP: A Benin wall hanging coexists with works by artists from the Ivory Coast and South Africa in Richard and Jeanne Presha's living room; the cube lamp is an Arthur Meckler design. The room itself is edged with a painted border taken from the 1920s pattern "Domino Series" by distinguished Swedish porcelain and ceramic designer Stig Lindberg.

BOTTOM: The black and chrome finish of this 1940s globe epitomizes the look of Machine-Age design, which the Preshas feel complements their African art.

OPPOSITE: The Preshas encounter a major dilemma over and over again—which classics to keep for themselves and which to include in their Philadelphia showroom gallery of early modern furniture of the 1930s, 1940s, and 1950s. They see a natural partnership between this furniture and the progressive character of carved, sculptural African design, and their home reflects this philosophy. The elements of their living room have international origins, blending the high-tech with the biomorphic; the Preshas have included, for example, a tubular-framed sofa and armchairs by Kem Weber; a glass-topped coffee table by Mies van der Rohe; and a dramatic zebra-patterned wool rug.

cases traditional woods and finishes in ebony, mahogany, and gold leaf. Even the walls and floor feature Egyptian-inspired geometric patterns. The combination conveys an unmistakable strength and drama.

Still other living rooms have drawn successfully from varied design options, fusing eclectic elements and imagery. They range from the sub-Saharan imagery of J. R. Sanders's living room in New York—whose chocolates, creams, golds, and beiges serve as a backdrop for his informal displays of art and collectibles from a number of regions—to Richard and Jeanne Presha's fusion of West African textiles and patterned furniture from the organic modern period of the 1930s and '40s. This union transcends cultural and design borders to play up contrasts and striking similarities.

Note the lack of African visual clichés—a heavy reliance on animal skins, for example—in all of the living rooms featured in this chapter. Similarly, these rooms show off African art and design in inventive ways: the homeowners here have no interest in perfectly coordinated color schemes, matching tone for tone or print for print.

Your own honest interpretations of African style are the keys to striking a harmonious balance of beauty and function in your home. Put simply, if it works for you, your guests are likely to find your interiors warm and inviting, too. With African style, traditional meets modern, East meets West, and the familiar and unfamiliar become one. The results are always exciting.

SHOWCASING YOUR PRIDE AND JOY

The living room will certainly receive much attention from collectors of African art, since this space usually offers the most impressive display possibilities. Because it generally has the greatest amount of wall area, the room can gracefully accommodate, say, quilts, raffia ceremonial skirts, or collections of textiles and paintings. And a living room often has fireplaces and architectural features not found elsewhere in the home. These architectural elements offer display options that can enhance art or objects, emphasizing their best features and details.

In some living rooms, new items are rookies that must earn the right to stand side by side with veteran treasures. For example, Helen Bershad, a painter who lives in Philadelphia and collects figurines, feels that any new acquisition must be able to hold its own next to the others in her collection: the design must be equally strong. But ask a collector why a particular piece of African art captured his eye, and he may offer any number of responses. He may note its historical sig-

OPPOSITE, CLOCKWISE FROM TOP LEFT: From the collection of Warren Robbins, these figurative Asante gold weights were cast in bronze by the "lost wax" process. Used to weigh gold dust, the principal exchange of Ghanaians from the 15th to the 20th centuries, they rested on one side of the scale while the gold was placed on the other. Gold weights, which often depicted local proverbs, were also used as symbols of status.

These contemporary hand-carved walking sticks were made by the Makonde people, who are known throughout East Africa for their distinct and fine sculptural traditions.

Part of a twin set, this sculptured head from the art deco period beautifully captures the softly molded features of a black woman.

From the Welsh-Asante collection, a Bamileke beaded sculpture from Cameroon is richly covered with cowrie shells. These shells were used as a traditional form of currency in some parts of Africa.

ABOVE: A close-up of contemporary African figures that Carolyn Tyler brought back from Africa. The symbol of the mother is a recurring theme through the history of African art.

nificance, its symbolism, origins, or rarity. Perhaps it was purely a visual attraction based on the beauty or design of the piece. Or maybe he just had to have it because it "feels right" for his home. Many collectors, after all, believe that the only things worth collecting are the things you love.

In collecting African art, enjoyment of the object is key. But our enjoyment sometimes results in a display that reveals our distance

BELOW: Personally meeting the artists whose work she owns, Carolyn Tyler, a television anchor in San Francisco, is a supportive and active patron of African-American art and design. Her home is filled with carved figures from West Africa, furniture by designer Cheryl Riley, and kilims from North Africa. Above her fireplace hangs a Joe Sam mixed-media piece, entitled *The Invisible Hunter.*

RIGHT, TOP: J. R. Sanders, an exhibit, graphics, and interior designer, lives in the center of Manhattan, but the feeling is African once he closes the door to his spacious Manhattan apartment. Beautifully carved guardian lions are an intriguing element of the massive carved chairs in his living room.

BOTTOM: The many shades of rich brown and the feel of straw, wood, and steerhide add a subtle intensity to Sanders' living room.

OPPOSITE: Sanders, originally from Kansas, has created a feeling of rustic elegance in his apartment, which is graced with high ceilings and tall windows. The subtle, monochromatic color scheme of rich earth tones, beiges, creams, coffee browns, and gold gives the interior a warm wash, while the velvety chevron-patterned furniture, an Egyptian coffee table with a loosely woven top, and a steerhide rug add to the mix of textures. Masks from Zaire and Mali, mudcloth pillows, and an Ethiopian food server tie it all together.

OPPOSITE: Looking down into the living room of Carlos Ascher, a rug dealer in Philadelphia, is like stepping into Morocco. The warmth of the sunken seating area in front of his fireplace is generated more from the lush layering of carpets than from the heat of the blaze.

ABOVE: Leather hassocks provide additional seating for guests at Ascher's town house. These ottomans are more detailed than most, but the designs nonetheless mix well with his rugs and other textiles.

THIS PAGE, TOP: These plates exemplify the combination of Egyptian and Greek patterns that characterize Empire designs. BOTTOM: A close-up of the carved figures enhanced with gold leaf on Prigent's Empire armchair. OPPOSITE: Mahogany, gold leaf, winged creatures, scarabs, and stars are among the many details that define Empire style. Together they form a rich and regal backdrop for a red satin Early Egyptian Revival armchair in Roger Prigent's living room.

from the original sources of this art. We may think nothing of placing an initiation mask from the Yoruba next to a mask used in ceremonial dances by the Hausa. Many Africans, however, would never dream of mixing masks used in different rituals by different groups. Each collector thus needs to resolve his or her own opinions on maintaining the original context of African art.

Another concern with collecting art is determining what would show it at its best. For example, a collection can take on added importance with a greater number of items. Some collectors want an army of masks gazing from a prominent wall in their living room, or they might want rows of mounted brass bracelets marching across an antique table. It is visually striking to have so many pieces assembled together, and the repetition of pattern draws attention to the design.

As the focal point of a living room, a fireplace—its mantel or the space above it—is ideal for displaying smaller art objects, paintings, and wall hangings. Shelving, built-in bookcases, and glassed-in cabinets are also excellent places for displaying small collectibles, grouped together to create a sense of unity and organization. Objects can be assembled with unrelated items to create intriguing compositions. What could have been an ordinary bookcase in the Armans'

ABOVE: Sheryl Ward leads a complicated life as television executive, chef, jewelry and furnishings designer, as well as wife and mother. But in her sunny San Francisco apartment, she takes an uncomplicated approach to living with African art and design. This means using clean, simple forms and organic materials such as leather, wood, and wrought iron. Mud-cloth pillows rest in a black leather butterfly chair. The leather sofa is draped with a West African strip weave. Atop a mirrored armoire from the 1930s are West and Central African masks and sculptures that encircle a portrait of a beloved relative.

TOP: Dr. Kariamu Welsh-Asante, professor of African-American Studies at Temple University, created an African-inspired collage for her wooden desk, with elephant bookends, a calabash gourd, a turquoise head by African-American artist Elizabeth Catlett, and a Tji Wara headdress by the Bamani of Mali, worn during dance ceremonies to inspire young farmers to produce healthy crops. The contemporary stool is from Ghana, carved with an Adinkra pattern known as Sankofa.
BOTTOM: What better place to make an escape with a good book or just to wind down at the end of the day than under a canopy decorated with a mud cloth from Mali. In his living room, Warren Robbins, founding director emeritus and senior scholar of the National Museum of African Art in Washington, D.C., added an elephant headdress from Cameroon for added protection. A curator, lecturer, writer, archivist, former teacher and diplomat, Robbins is known to many as "the collector."
Indeed, his Washington town house is a collector's paradise, where Picasso and Matisse proudly join company with African art.

RIGHT: Deborah Johnson's door is dressed for company with a skirt of beads and cowrie shells, Kuba cloth, and a whisk broom. Her collection of West African masks, an iron candelabra, and mud-cloth pillows add textural richness to her living room.

OPPOSITE: In Maureen Zarember's sitting room, a Cameroonian stool becomes a table base to hold a beaded basket, a stack of books, and the iron coils that were once used for currency in Zaire. The Asante chair at left is a seat of prestige; it is made of wood and leather, with brass tacks and finials. Behind it stands a strikingly patterned Bamileke masquerade mask with elephant ears from Cameroon.

home, for instance, is made attractive with the addition of African sculpture.

An end table or coffee table can be the perfect stage for displaying dramatic figures, pottery, baskets, masks, and small objects such as gold weights and jewelry. For example, Roger Prigent created an eye-catching still life by contrasting a Greek bust with African heads, alongside other relics on a tabletop in his living room. And Veronica Robertson of New York assembled a popular African game, pieces of sculpture, a bowl of fruit, dried flowers, and art books on a black lacquered table in her living room.

Your own collections of African and African-inspired art can offer pleasure to your family and guests. These objects may come with fascinating stories of origin from past owners, or they may have fulfilled some vital role in a village household. No matter how large or small, formal or casual, expensive or modest, your assemblages will radiate warmth because they are favored and loved. Surround yourself with them and display them at their very best.

OPPOSITE: Understated yet unmistakably African elements add flavor to this contemporary setting designed by the authors for Philadelphia textile dealer Tahira Amatullah. The goal for this interior was simplicity, with plenty of calming curves and fluid forms. Showcasing a variety of traditional African textiles, the loft features early modern pieces like the Eames black molded plywood chair and an elliptical table that is a Charles Eames knockoff from Richard and Jeanne Presha's collection; the area rug reflects the form of this table in its blue shield-like shapes.

THIS PAGE, TOP: Marrying traditional African design with modern Western elements can create such beautiful combinations as the royal blue Ghanaian Kente used with more contemporary prints from the Ivory Coast and a Matisse-inspired fabric. The whimsical lines of the 1950s lamp, a flea market find, works well with the vibrant textiles.

BOTTOM: A hand-carved Senufo bench keeps company with the Charles Eames molded plywood chair; the two complement each other because of their shared sculptural grace.

While Africa is not widely known for having an extensive furniture culture, it is home to the oldest: the archaeological record reveals that Africans have been making wooden furniture since at least 3100 B.C. Through the ages, African furniture has been skillfully designed, intricately handcrafted with innovative patterns and motifs, and often made from rare and exotic woods. Some early pieces even featured gold leaf, veneers, and inlays. With such careful attention paid to aesthetics as well as function, the work falls comfortably into the categories of both fine art and applied art, or utilitarian design.

FURNITURE FORMS

The earliest specimens of furniture known to us are from Egypt, and they are among the most elaborate. These furniture remains not only tell us about the level of technology existing in North Africa at the time, but also provide insight into lifestyles and functional needs of the past. Many items survived to the present more or less intact, because of Egypt's exceedingly dry climate and because of their entombment with the highest dignitaries of that ancient civilization. Religious beliefs in life after death dictated that material luxuries be provided for the departed's use in his or her future life, and

FURNITURE FORMS

OPPOSITE TOP: The solid walnut stools by Charles and Ray Eames are wonderful examples of modern design evocative of African art traditions. OPPOSITE BOTTOM: A handcarved Ghanaian stool features a Sankofa design. THIS PAGE, LEFT: Born in 1801, Thomas Day was a free black who became famous as a cabinetmaker. He designed and manufactured this stunning secretary with Sankofa patterns. THIS PAGE, RIGHT: A vibrant chest of drawers is by Maxime de la Falaise, a contemporary fashion and furniture designer.

FURNITURE FORMS

so great quantities of furniture were discovered in Egyptian burial sites, thereby creating a window to the past.

The tombs contained furniture enjoyed primarily by the upper classes, including tables, stools, chairs, beds, and storage chests of various shapes and sizes. These time capsules also held elegant armchairs and what we now call Egyptian-style beds, with footboards but no headboards, and large collapsible canopies. One example of exquisite design and craftsmanship is an armchair of Queen Hetepheres that was covered in gold sheathing and inlays, with carved lions' legs as supports. Although these pieces conveyed important social and ceremonial messages, they were designed to meet functional demands as well, and reveal fine craftsmanship even when compared to today's standards. The furniture from King Tutankhamen's tomb, for example, is considered more refined than anything produced in Europe from the beginning of the Dark Ages through the 18th century. It is also interesting to find that such elements as animal leg supports and animal feet were design details characteristic of the dynastic period, circa 3100 to 2700 B.C., although many people today associate these elegant features with the work of highly skilled 18th-century European cabinetmakers.

Other parts of Africa saw different developments in the design and use of furniture. For example, the Berbers and Moors of the Sahara and surrounding regions as well as the Masai of East Africa traditionally lived nomadic lives, moving with their herds in search of fresh grazing lands. Although furniture is better suited to a sedentary existence, these groups devised pieces that worked for a life on the move and that reflected their relationship with the earth. Woven mats, pillows, rugs, and light stools could be used for sitting, dining, cooking, socializing, working, and sleeping in different places at different times, especially when these activities occurred at or near ground level.

Religious beliefs played a role in limiting the production of furniture in Africa. "African spiritual beliefs hold that all things in the natural world are part of the Cosmos and therefore all things belong to God," explains Dr. Kariamu Welsh-Asante. "Trees, which are part of

ABOVE: A collection of headrests from East Africa displays a dazzling variety in design, with some far more elaborate than others. Clockwise from top are headrests from the Sudan, Kenya, Tanzania, Zimbabwe, and Mozambique.

nature, were considered sacred, to be worshiped. Therefore, one did not just cut down a tree to produce something like a chest or chair." Instead, the stools, masks, and other objects made from wood were often designed not for utilitarian reasons but with special, sacred purposes in mind: for honoring kings, for offering prayers, or for worshiping deities.

SEATS OF POWER, SEATS OF PURPOSE

How often have we heard someone say, "This is *my* chair," staking claim to a special seat that seems to take on the occupant's personality as well as his or her contours? In Africa, it would be a stool that is similarly associated with a specific individual, whose presence and place are maintained even if that person steps away from it for

TOP: This low, four-legged stool that is almost saddlelike in form is from the Dinka people of the Sudan.

LEFT: The wisdom knot stool produced in Ghana is accompanied by the expression, "Only the wise can undo the knot."

TOP RIGHT: The "Bakuba Griffin" dining table, designed by Cheryl Riley, features a hand-painted top reminiscent of the weaving and painting traditions of the Kuba people of Zaire. The supports are lion-clawed legs, inspired by the book *Where the Wild Things Are* by Maurice Sendak.

BOTTOM RIGHT: New York stylist Robert Teszar chose his Senufo bed for its simplicity of form.

a period of time. Throughout the continent, stools carry great aesthetic, functional, and ceremonial importance. Not only is the stool an emblem of the maker's creative flair and the owner's identity, it also plays an integral role in nearly all activities, from daily household duties to elaborate ceremonies honoring royalty.

Stools were traditionally created for village chiefs and were regarded as symbols of authority. But the stool is at home with all people in Africa, whether they are great or humble, pastoral farmers or urban dwellers. Stools communicate power, status, gender, moral values, and beliefs. Some stools are objects of worship; in the Akan and Ga religious ceremonies in West Africa, they were even "fed" and "given drink." Others are presented to women to celebrate a marriage or the birth of a child. There are stools for men and stools for women, stools for kings and stools for queen mothers, stools for chiefs as well as for their subchiefs, and even stools for a king's stool bearer, each with a design that communicates a meaning.

One very renowned stool belongs to the Asante of Ghana. This golden stool, known as "Sika Gwa Kofi," symbolizes national sovereignty and dates back to the establishment of the Asante confederacy at the end of the 17th century. It is said to have fallen from the heavens, landing at the feet of Okomfo Anokye, who then became the "Asantehene," or king of the Asante. The golden stool is not meant for actual sitting, since it is said to contain the "Kra," or soul, of the original ancestor. As the real ruler of the Asante, it remains in the private possession of the reigning king, who protects it and derives his power through it.

While the chairs, couches, tables, and beds of Africa have in some ways been influenced by European and Islamic cultures, the traditional stool is essentially an indigenous design. Because they are often carved from a single piece of wood, African stools have a strong sculptural quality, which makes them resemble art more than furniture. And in many ways, they are art. It is this strong visual impact, as well as their charm and personality, that makes stools a favorite in Western interiors. Some collectors treat them as sculpture; others as a beautiful resting place for bodies, objets d'art, or maybe for a throw. The

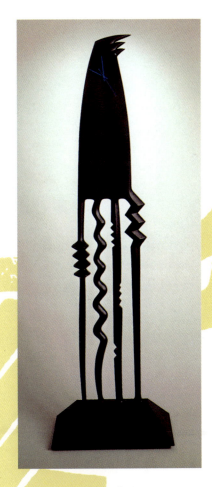

ABOVE: Furniture designer Peter Pierobon of Philadelphia created "Fetish," a clock in ebonized mahogany. Its painted hands take a functional element and give it a primordial gestural identity.

ABOVE: Made of rosewood, this stool by French designer Pierre Legrain was inspired by the sculpture traditions of West Africa. Working in Paris in the 1920s, Legrain used diverse woods in his pieces, including beechwood inlaid with mother-of-pearl, limed African oak, palm wood, and ebony.

basic design is simple but encompasses elegant lines, an organic and functional form, generous proportions, and powerful carved surfaces.

Generally, stools are quite low to the ground and have arcing seats and sculptural frames. The seat of the typical Asante stool, for example, is sculpted into a swayed arc, with a flat base without nuts, bolts, screws, or any other hardware. A stool's body, or supports, are sometimes straight and sometimes curved outwardly. It is here that the design of the stool takes off in various directions: there are as many different styles of Asante stools, for instance, as there are chiefs, and the symbols are endlessly varied.

The body of a Ga sovereignty stool might feature an antelope standing atop an elephant, conveying the message "The top is reached by wisdom, never by size." A support with a carved knot would mean "Only the wise can undo a wise knot." Stools from Tanzania, Kenya, Ethiopia, and other East African countries tend to be minimalist in their designs. They have bowl-like seats and often three legs that flare at the bottom, although some are designed with a single central support. Meanwhile, Cameroonian stools have intricately carved supports, often depicting animals, faces, and heads.

The best-known Senufo stool is the wash stool, which has a curved seat and four massive leg supports that are tapered at the bottom. Women along the Ivory Coast balanced these multifunctional stools upside down on their heads, the wash of the day nestled among the stool supports. Once they reached their destination, they would then use the stool as a seat while doing their wash. The fullness of the leg supports gives Senufo stools a feeling of power, yet they also have a playful quality, reminiscent of the rounded characters of a Botero painting. These are seats of power that will never topple!

FROM EMPIRE TO DECO

The glorification of Napoleon's military victories in Egypt and the stylized depiction of Egyptian symbols are hallmarks of the Empire period in European furniture design. This style was launched when, after his

BELOW: Just as Fauvist painters were drawn to new interpretations of African design, Maxime de la Falaise fuses European furnishings with traditional African design and painting techiques. With its unpretentious lines, a Scandinavian sideboard is a natural base for this unexpected aesthetic mating.

RIGHT: Cheryl Riley's style influences are global and while her "Talking Head" cabinet was inspired by ceremonial masks from New Guinea, she feels it shares kindred spirits with the African mask.

OPPOSITE: French designer Pierre Legrain, whose works celebrated the progressive spirit of West and Central African sculpture, designed this low table in 1925. The tabletop, with its angled ends, is covered in a rich brown snakeskin and rests on two massive snakeskin and nickelplated supports that are mounted on a nickelplated base. Legrain's remarkable designs have survived over the decades in private collections around the world.

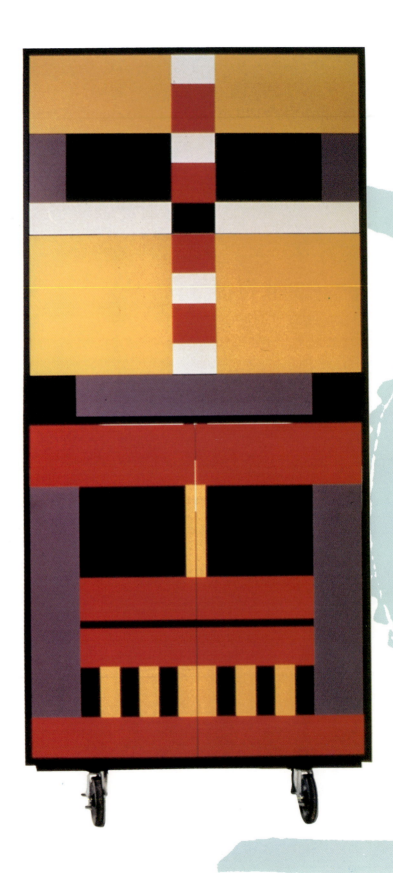

return from battles against the Ottomans in Egypt in 1799, Napoleon commissioned French cabinetmakers to design majestic furnishings to commemorate his travels.

The work was characterized by military symbols, such as arrows, spears, torches, and amulets. And for the first time, European furniture was embellished with Egyptian imagery such as the sphinx, winged griffins, pyramids, papyrus, palms, and scarabs, produced in ebony

and other tropical woods of Africa, with ornate mahogany veneers and gold sheathing. Campaign furniture—folding tables, chairs, and beds—designed for men traveling the battlefields and living outdoors also entered the European design lexicon, inspired in part by the folding furniture designed for celestial travel that was frequently found in Egyptian tombs. As the Empire style developed, it became more elaborate with, for instance, sofas shaped like Egyptian boats, complete with crocodile feet.

As the colonization of West Africa continued in the 19th century, ever-increasing quantities of African art arrived in Europe. By the turn of the century, traditional stools and chairs were beginning to influence the works of European furniture designers. Many designers of

the Art Deco period, for example, moved in the same circles as the Cubist, Fauvist, and German Expressionist painters who were looking to Africa for new ideas to explore in their artwork. It is easy to see how the artists' enthusiasm for all things African was transmitted to designers of home furnishings.

Inspired in part by the creative spirit of non-European cultures, Art Deco was influenced not only by African art but also by South American images. Aztec motifs, for example, were popularized by novels like *The Plumed Serpent* by D. H. Lawrence. The infusion of such elements into traditional European art during the Deco period revolutionized furniture and textile design. These influences produced Art Deco's brilliant colors, exotic finishes, and geometric shapes, and resulted in the wide use of ivory, animal skins, tropical woods, pyramidal shapes, and

BELOW: The Nefertiti office chair designed by Cheryl Riley takes advantage of modern technology to reinterpret ancient Egyptian designs. This regal classic chair is based on the folding designs found in the tombs of early Egyptian dignitaries.

OPPOSITE: Alex Locadia calls this design "Entertainment Console II." Combining such disparate materials as mahogany, brass, glass, and African artifacts makes his pieces a strong focal point in any room.

BELOW: The "Luba Yoruba" wooden chest has beaded bands around its feet; it was designed in 1994 by Cheryl Riley.

OPPOSITE: Another Riley piece is the coin-encrusted Tudor Table, made of wood with copper-sheathed supports.

motifs such as stylized birds and rays of the sun. The Cubist and Futurist characteristics of Art Deco textiles and wallpapers reflected the abstract style of African patterns. Simple lines, a balance of volume and color, refined proportions, functional restraint, and angular, abstract patterns were all highlighted, replacing the ornate, often florid furnishings of the earlier Art Nouveau period.

The best known of the African-inspired furniture designers of the era include Pierre Legrain, Marcel Coard, and Emile-Jacques Ruhlmann. Legrain, the most innovative and important of them, began as a bookbinder and later became a decorator and furniture designer. In the early 1920s, he collaborated with Jacques Doucet, a wealthy connoisseur and collector of the arts, on Doucet's Paris residence. The designer, who strived for inventive forms with minimal yet dramatic detail, placed African-inspired pieces against the backdrop of Doucet's collection of works by Modigliani, Matisse, Picasso, and Miró, and by unknown African artists and sculptors. Inspired by the stools and chairs of the Ivory Coast and the Congo, by wooden neck rests from Egypt, and by Asante gold weights cast as miniature seats, Legrain created a mélange that recalled the texture and hues of Africa.

Drawing upon the multiplicity of woods used in African art as well as its lines and details, Legrain's furniture designs included an ebony and palisander drum table with supports carved in African motifs; Cubist red and blue leather armchairs with trapezoidal backs and high angular arms; a rectangular low table with nickel plating and brown snakeskin; a bench of limed African oak, ebony, and gold lacquer; a stool in black lacquer and shagreen; and an ebony-veneered stool inlaid with mother-of-pearl. Most of Legrain's African-inspired works designed for Doucet still exist and are considered masterpieces with great provenance.

In the 1920s and '30s, Art Deco was extremely popular in the United States as well, and many of its stylistic tendencies evolved into the modern designs of the 1940s and '50s. In America, a variety of new technologies enabled such furniture designers as Eero Saarinen and Charles Eames to experiment with sleek, minimalist lines. Techniques for bonding wood, rubber, and glass or casting metal made it possible to create the hallmark features of modern furniture: a biomorphic appearance, molded frames, angled and tapered legs, and pointed feet, characteristics similar to and influenced by organically sculptured African furniture.

Today, a growing number of furniture designers are once again pointing their inspirational compasses to Africa; their ranks include Tony Whitfield in New York, Cedric Williams in Columbus, and Richard Bennett in Detroit, to name a few. In these pages, for example, you will see

copper tables encrusted with Nigerian coins by Cheryl Riley of San Francisco, a shieldlike bench in black leather by Alex Locadia of New York, and a funky Egyptian-inspired bed made of African ribbon mahogany and brushed aluminum by Courtney Sloane of Jersey City.

it

is no wonder that we are drawn to the kitchen: it is the heart of the home, where labors of love are carried out every day. Entering a kitchen full of rich aromas, replete with fresh vegetables and fruits, herbs and spices, collections of colorful ceramic platters, baskets and bowls, and plenty of shining pots and pans, is one of the great pleasures of life, one that can evoke the warmest memories of family gatherings

kitchens and dining rooms

and special meals. It is here that the connection can most lovingly be made between body and soul.

In Africa, the kitchen can be part of a house, a separate building, an open-sided thatched hut with more than one hearth, or an outdoor space—which is often the case in equatorial nations where the climate is hot and steamy. But here, too, the kitchen is more than simply a place for cooking food; it is a place where legacies are passed from one generation to the next. The hearth, fire, and heat of this

place symbolize the radiant spirit of the family, clan, and village, explains Dr. Theophile Obenga, professor of African Studies at Temple University in Philadelphia. As a center of communication, it is also here that women and young people share the daily happenings of the village and exchange updates on crops, notes on the children, and other important news.

Where there is little formal schooling, the kitchen is often a place of education: life's lessons are taught there while meals are being prepared. Amid pots, pans, calabashes, gourds, and pottery, the young learn moral values, traditions, and many of the skills they will need as adults. And as is the case still in many parts of the world, the kitchen in Africa is a woman's domain. It is the headquarters of the women of a family, a place where they conduct their business. Men typically stay out of the way as women provide nourishment for the future in every way imaginable.

African mealtime is always a family affair; from beginning to end it is a gathering that includes grandparents, aunts, uncles, nephews, nieces, and cousins. Yet no matter how many people are expected, there is always enough for an extra person, who will certainly be made

PRECEDING PAGE: "Altar No. 2," a mixed-media art work from Barbara Jane Bullock's "Healer" series, hangs in her Philadelphia kitchen above her colorful dishes, which are stored on open shelves. Calabash gourds, baskets, and whisk brooms adorn a corner wall, along with a collection of wooden spoons. A piece of Kente cloth draped over a radiator contributes to the riot of color, while a shopping basket provides a subtle, textural contrast.
OPPOSITE: Step into Bullock's kitchen and step into an African marketplace, splashed with color and filled with all sorts of odds and ends. Anthropomorphic light switches squirm on the walls; animal figures roam on furniture and windowsills; and baskets, brooms, and calabash gourds sprout all over the place. A lizard struts his stuff on the edge of one of the hand-painted chairs, and the table is covered with a South African Pakhamani textile.
TOP: A blending of contemporary and traditional tableware comes together for beautiful function.
LEFT: A rainbow of dishes bearing African motifs stands in a wooden drain tray.

103

OPPOSITE AND ABOVE: In Margreet Monster's Victorian home, large windows bring the outdoors in. Nature gets an extra boost with indigenous plants from Africa including agapanthus, lily of the Nile from Egypt, and clivia from South Africa. The ceramic tiles, produced by Cerillos Ceramics in Philadelphia, evoke West African symbols and patterns; Monster's table is covered with a Pakhamani cloth from South Africa.

to feel part of the family and fed as if there were no tomorrow. In village life, cooperation is vital, and the well-being and cohesion of the extended family are of utmost value. Every man and woman is responsible for the well-being of the children in the village, and this very close union is most often strengthened around the cooking fires.

WARMING THE HEART OF THE HOME

In our fast-paced world, there is something to be said for focusing on the heart of the home. The natural warmth of the kitchen provides a welcome transition from the outside world, and the design of this space has become even more inviting in recent years as its importance has grown. There is no better way to enhance this natural warmth than by infusing a kitchen with African elements.

Close your eyes and imagine the excited voices of an African family that has prepared an elaborate meal for guests from far away. Think of the symbolism of coming together to share a rice dish in a generous bowl; conjure up the aroma of cloves in Zanzibar, the golden hue and unmistakable flavor of passionfruit juice, the texture of the fufu, or mashed yams, or the familiarity of suka ma wiki, collard

OPPOSITE: Sheryl Ward confides, "I have a weakness for chairs of all kinds." Here are two of her most recent additions, which she has customized with a fresh coat of paint, decorative patterns and leopard seats. She adds to her dining room bright candles in holders that seem to ask a question while evoking images of Adinkra symbols, and colorful baskets and textiles to create an interpretation of African style that is light and whimsical.

LEFT: Joe Sam and Donna Bellorado's kitchen is a welcoming setting for some of his art work as well as for African dolls and a delightful side chair of jumbo proportions created by his daughter, Joeonna. To the left of the china hutch is Sam's mixed-media piece representing China; standing on the right of the hutch is "David" with his slingshot, from the San Francisco artist's "Black Bible Series." The figure hanging to the right is called "Hide and Go Seek," and is a small-scale version of one in a series of 12-foot figures created for Los Angeles's mass transit system.

107

RIGHT: Color, form, and pattern define the look of Richard and Jeanne Presha's dining room. The chairs were designed by Joe Atkinson and manufactured by Thonet. Above the mantelpiece hangs a print in honor of Josephine Baker, whose popularity surged in the Europe of the 1920s just as African art and design were making inroads there.

OPPOSITE: Designed and produced by Armand P. Arman for the family's Manhattan loft apartment, these dining tables and chairs were inspired by the form of string instruments and create a visual rhythm of their own. The extensive collection of sculptured figures, produced by the Kota and the Obamba peoples of Gabon, offers an extraordinary display of stylistic originality and exquisite craftsmanship. The painting on the rear wall is an original Arman piece, while the masks are from West and Central Africa. Add to this the Japanese Samurai helmets and the room fairly explodes with art.

greens' African cousin. These images and sensations can be evoked in your kitchen and dining room through the use of color, textiles, basketry, and art objects. There are myriad exciting ideas for making the imagery of Africa manifest in a rich and distinctive design. But remember, the true spirit of Africa lies not so much in the visual impact of collectibles brought back from a vacation or in elaborate African-inspired home furnishings, but rather in the pleasure they give you, both decoratively and functionally.

Whether your kitchen has a country rustic or urban contemporary feeling, African household objects can add interest. Don't be fooled by their good looks; these objects have a purpose and were designed for daily kitchen use. So bring your collection of East African baskets out of storage or pick up a few if you have none. Clay pots and baskets are perfect for storing everything from spices to firewood; use them to display fresh fruits and vegetables that need not be refrigerated. Gourds, cut from the calabash plant, carved in the form of bowls and engraved with beautiful patterns, are particularly useful for preparing or serving food. Turkanar milk containers work well as wine chillers, while colorful North African tiles can serve as trivets to absorb heat.

OPPOSITE: The color palette of the forties and fifties complements the African objects in Richard and Jeanne Presha's kitchen. The textile on the table is a flat-weave blanket from Mali; the tangerine-colored armchair is a molded plastic design by Charles Eames and Ray Eames. LEFT, TOP: William Karg is a leading New York collector and dealer of contemporary African art representing such artists as Charles Sekano of South Africa. In the dining room of his brownstone, Karg creates quiet drama through the minimal lines and subtle curve of the dining chairs tucked beneath a black cherry wood table, the elegant form of Ethiopian chairs against the walls, the beautiful design of a Moroccan food preserver, and the contemporary works by Ethiopian artists Kunder Boghossian and Tesfaye Tessima. LEFT, BOTTOM: A collection of West African pedestal bowls and fifties-inspired ceramics provide contrast to a commercially produced African textile runner.

Display is an important part of the African-inspired kitchen. Since even the simplest bowl or container has something special about it, these unique kitchenwares deserve to be showcased.

Once you have established the focal points in your kitchen, other elements can play supporting roles. Turn textiles into hand towels, tablecloths, and window treatments that are consistent with the feeling you are creating. Consider a backsplash of Moroccan tiles, or indigo-painted walls, or a stenciled motif to crown your kitchen.

ON THE TABLE

Never before have china, ceramics, and table textiles with African-inspired motifs and color combinations been so widely available, offering exciting opportunities to integrate authentic African crafts and furnishings with homegrown versions. For example, the wide diversity of pottery and ceramic styles throughout the African continent can give rise to all kinds of interpretations. These new styles in tableware range from casual contemporary designs for everyday use to sophisticated formal patterns. Some maintain a strict adherence to traditional designs, such as the Ghanaian Kente cloth–inspired pieces; others borrow unrelated motifs and mix them in whimsical fashion, while still others are more experimental, fusing African symbols with various modern design elements.

Platters, bowls, and tureens in solid complementary colors will support this look and complete your table setting, bringing a certain calm to an already striking tablescape. The common spirit of African and African-influenced pieces pulls them together and makes for beautiful partnerships. In the kitchen of Philadelphians Margreet and Willem Monster, for example, colors and patterns play out brilliantly in the contrast of geometric china designed by Harris-Roberts for Swid Powell and an authentic hand-painted Pakhamani tablecloth produced by Zulu women of South Africa. While the china pattern is not necessarily African in origin, it makes a perfect mate for the fabric.

Since textiles play such a pivotal role in the spirit of Africa, they can add verve to your table as to any room of your home. Jeanne and Richard Presha of New York have mixed furniture from the 1940s and '50s with African-inspired design elements. For special occasions, they drape a cotton flat-weave textile from Mali across their dinner table. The pattern and color of this textile strike a fine balance with an early modern Charles Eames plastic molded armchair as well as a Scandinavian-designed wall unit. The liveliness of the textile is also

LEFT: Cheryl Riley's "Zanzibar Table" mirrors the configuration of the island in silver leaf hand-painted on the tabletop. Her studded "Starburst Chair" is from her "Circle Suite" series. Resting on the table is a Suku-style helmet mask from Zaire and a nail-studded double-headed dog, a Kongo power figure from Zaire. In the background is Riley's "Hunter Screen," which was inspired by shirts worn by the Bamana of Mali to ensure safe return from hunting expeditions; attached to the screen are protective objects such as mirrors to reflect back evil spirits and pouches containing protective trinkets. OPPOSITE, TOP: Detail of Riley's unusual helmet mask from Zaire. OPPOSITE, BOTTOM: Detail of the "Hunter Screen."

reflected in the displayed assortment of kitchen regalia, which shares many of the same colors.

Printed cloths produced in Africa for export are now plentiful, and they come in a variety of styles and color combinations. You can find tablecloths, runners, napkins, and place mats in these patterns, or you can purchase the fabric and make the items yourself. The export fabrics are generally machine-washable, but if your table is draped with authentic textiles and you're concerned about food stains, add a runner, mats, or some type of overlay.

Keep in mind that there's no single formula for a beautiful kitchen or table. Some of these ideas may fit your kitchen; some may not. African style is hands-on: it challenges your creative resourcefulness and invites you to explore the spirit of Africa in personal ways.

Masks and sculptural figures typically come to mind when someone mentions African art. However, fine art exists throughout the continent in the form of body decorations, jewelry, textiles, basketry, pottery, and furniture. As with any art, in order to appreciate its complexity and aesthetics, we must explore the meaning of African work: where did it come from, who created it, what are its social ramifications. And we must keep in mind that art means one thing to the artist and another to the viewer. In the home, it can serve as a visual and spiritual focal point, but its form and beauty can be appreciated even in isolation.

ART AND OBJECTS

From prehistoric days, craftsmen in Africa displayed a sense of beauty and symmetry in making the most utilitarian of objects, including knives, pottery, vessels, pins, and combs fashioned from bones and shells. The earliest known decorative art was made by the Egyptians of the Old Kingdom from 2700 to 2200 B.C., who carved large images of their gods or rulers in stone, wood, and copper. They were skilled jewelers who made beads, necklaces, bracelets, and crowns, using gold, silver, and precious stones; these luxuries were placed in delicate boxes fashioned from wood and sometimes trimmed in gold.

ABOVE: These brass geometric Asante gold weights reveal the influence of the Islamic faith, which prohibits figurative symbols. They are part of the private collection of Warren Robbins.

Throughout much of the African continent, however, art has traditionally meant functional art. Among the myriad masterpieces are such objects of everyday life as gourds, bowls, stools, snuff containers, walking sticks, baskets, jewelry, textiles, and headrests. These items are not only functional but beautiful as well, embellished by carving, applied stones, jewels, beads, paint, raffia, or simply by the rich luster of the material used.

Although these utilitarian objects were often decorated for personal pleasure, the creative techniques used were deeply rooted in tradition. A long apprenticeship was often required in order to pass on the technical knowledge to create them. Within his or her community, the artist was almost as important as a shaman or chieftain in conveying religious and magical beliefs, and the hidden message in a piece was often more important than its surface beauty.

Certain areas were and still are known as centers for a particular craft or industry. For example, Asante stools are produced from odum trees that grow in and around Kumasi, the ancient Asante center of trade, commerce, and education in Ghana. Kente or narrow strip weaving is a specialty in the villages of Wonoo and Bonwire in Ghana, while soapstone objects are plentiful near Kisumu on Lake Victoria in Kenya. Makonde carvings can be found in eastern Tanzania, and some parts of Botswana are known for their baskets.

Whatever form it took, African art reflected the beliefs of a group rather than those of an individual. This resulted in pieces that reveal the religious and social importance of plants, animals, and other natural elements. Human renderings also expressed communal beliefs: for example, the Ife and Nok cultures of 200 B.C., which are linked ancestrally, created sculpture with massive heads in keeping with their belief that the head is the center of life.

THE ELEMENTS OF AFRICAN ART

While it varies from region to region, sculpture is indeed the best-known form of African art, and among the commonly collected works are figurines, ceremonial regalia, and masks. During the 19th century, artists, soldiers, missionaries, and merchants brought African masks to Europe. For many, these masks captured the sense of excitement and adventure promised by an exotic continent. As noted earlier, European artists in particular were deeply influenced by African masks: artists such as Picasso saw in them a freedom of expression that took risks and stretched aesthetic possibilities in new and unimagined ways. Elements that are characteristic of African art began to surface in European art, especially among the avant-garde. The works of

ABOVE: This hand-carved chess set was produced by artist Joe Sam. After creating this interracial chess set, he buried the pieces for a year so that Mother Nature could apply the finishing touch of patina.

TOP LEFT: Sheryl Ward's prized possessions are the West African iron and brass bracelets, rings, and anklets that line her fireplace mantel. Some were worn for adornment; others contain bells or pebbles and were worn for dancing.

TOP MIDDLE: These bracelets, from the collection of Warren Robbins, were created by Ndebele women of South Africa, who are known for their beadwork as well as for the striking geometric patterns they paint on the exterior walls of their houses.

TOP RIGHT: A light-colored wooden bracelet stands out from darker ones in Maureen Zarember's collection.

BOTTOM AND OPPOSITE: A Kanaga mask from the Dogon people hangs behind the spinning wheel in Barbara Carter-Mitchell's living room. Together, they cast intriguing shadows on the wall.

ABOVE: African flowers are grouped with Taurey figures from West Africa to create an intriguing still life.

Modigliani, for example, suggest characteristics found in Fang masks from Gabon, with eyebrows as parallel lines, long faces, oval eyes, and tiny mouths.

There are basically three types of African masks: those worn over the face, like the flat geometric shapes of the Bakota in Gabon; those worn on top of the head, such as the Tji Wara antelope figures created by the Bambara of Mali; and those that fit over the entire head, such as the black helmet masks worn by Mende women during initiation ceremonies in Sierra Leone. Some masks are enormous; the

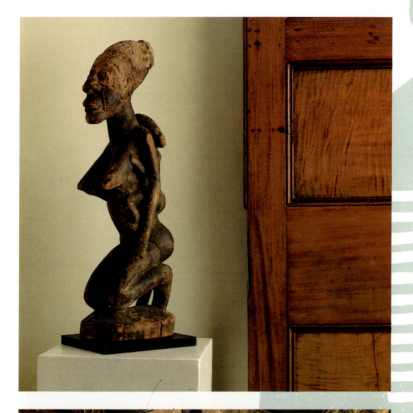

TOP: This Yoruba sculpture makes a strong statement placed next to the richly textured pocket door at the Philadelphia home of painter Helen Bershad and her husband, Jack. Because mothers are considered calm, just, and giving, the image of a mother with a child on her back is a common one on carvings offered as thanks to a deity or on those requesting a wish.

BOTTOM: The Armans' reliquary or funeral figures are extraordinary examples of stylistic originality and exquisite craftsmanship. Created by the Kota and Obamba of Gabon, they have a wood core with a copper or brass overlay.

ABOVE: Textile dealer Veronica Robertson creates an interesting still life on her black lacquer table with a traditional game played throughout Africa, a bowl of fruit, dried flowers, illustrated books, and African figures.

Dogon in Mali, for example, have masks that are 6 feet in height.

In all their different variations, masks are made for many purposes: to oversee burial rites, punish offenders, honor royalty, ensure good weather and crops, or commemorate marriages and births. They are imbued with the supernatural powers of ancestors and of nature spirits, which are called upon during ceremonies. For example, Baga dancers in coastal Guinea carried massive Nimba masks on their shoulders to capture the attention of the goddess of fertility.

INVOKING THE SPIRITS

Africans have produced exquisite carvings for years, particularly in the savannas and rain forests, where ebony and other trees are in abundance; these figures have also been made of terra-cotta and bronze. While carvers generally re-created the traditional forms that had been passed down through the ages, they nevertheless used imagination and skill to create signature pieces. Some of their peers could simply look at an item and immediately identify the maker.

The imagery found in figurines is often highly specific. Mother and child pairs are common motifs, and were typically intended to ensure fertility. But this image is also associated with royalty. For example, in Cameroon, a king in the grass fields was installed only after one of his wives gave birth; at the end of this waiting period, the figure of a mother and child was carved to commemorate the beginning of the king's new life.

LEFT: "When God created Africa, he was just showing off," says Joe Sam, a painter, sculptor, and mixed-media artist, who lives with his wife, Donna Bellorado, and their daughter, Joeonna, in a three-story house on Petrero Hill in San Francisco. With creative resourcefulness paralleling that of the African artisan, assemblages of any manner of found objects can find their way to his canvases, which often combine African, American Indian, and South Pacific masks, sculptures, and dolls. To the left of the window are three of Sam's early works; another is on wheels in the foreground.

In some areas of Nigeria, the figure of a man and wife symbolizes the economic and social bonds that are created between two extended families, as well as by a couple, in marriage. Then there are the *minkisi* of the Bakongo, a group concentrated in Zaire, northwest Angola, and the People's Republic of the Congo. Minkisi essentially means "things that do things." Spirits were embodied in the minkisi, which could be pots, shells, small bundles, or wooden figures, and were called upon to ease the pain of droughts, slavery, epidemics, poverty, and other sufferings.

Figures along the Ivory Coast include the Baules' "Other World" women and men. Linking the real world to the imaginary one of dreams, these round wooden figures serve as reminders of milestones in life, from marriages to births to deaths. They also serve as fantasy mates who are rivals to living partners, often compensating for their weaknesses.

THE ARTS OF ROYALTY

Serving as emblems of authority, ceremonial regalia include crowns, staffs, stools, and gongs. Rings, bracelets, pendants, and earrings can also be included in this category, with some designs so large or so elaborate that they could hinder movement. Whether carved or cast, these items were often elaborately detailed and finely crafted; gold, silver, bronze, and brass were used as precious metals suitable for kings and queens.

Royal courts of the Asante in Ghana in particular made spectacular use of gold. It was found everywhere, from chairs to umbrellas and from breastplates to castanets. Some of the gold was pure, but a good portion was recycled with other metals to create what is known as fetish gold. To complement their trade in gold, the Asante produced weights made of gold and bronze that were often in the form of humans or birds; these too are prized collectibles.

LEFT: Carolyn Tyler's impressive collection of masks, brought back from her visits to various regions in Africa, is grouped for strong impact.

OPPOSITE: Crisscrossing the Atlantic for both business and pleasure, Drs. Kariamu and Molefe Welsh-Asante have traveled to African villages making acquaintances with artists and craftsmen to see for themselves how traditions of art and design play a part in everyday life. Both professors of African-American Studies at Temple University, the couple carefully selects additions to their home. A painting by Kenyan artist Adhiambo provides a colorful backdrop for their sculpture collection, which includes a Dogon carving of an elder smoking a pipe and a helmet mask from Burkina Faso, both on the table. From left against the wall: a Yoruba female figure; a beaded Bamileke sculpture produced for the king's court in the Cameroons; another Yoruba woman; and a large Baganimba mask used in ceremonial fertility dances.

UTILITARIAN OBJECTS

Items of everyday use—stools, bowls, plates, cups, jugs, baskets, headrests, gourds, and walking sticks—were embellished as much as those intended for ritual use. Often lightweight and portable, these diverse objects shared a unique combination of form and function, tradition and personal creativity. So exquisitely detailed was the craftsmanship that it was not uncommon for the pieces to be buried with their owners.

Baskets, for example, are still woven today using centuries-old techniques. Intended for myriad purposes, baskets are primarily used to carry such things as clothing and wood or to store food and other items. Some are so tightly woven that they can be used to hold water. Wood, gourds, and animal hides can be attached to them as well. Gourds made from calabashes that have been hollowed out and dried are also popular vessels. And both baskets and gourds serve as decorative items.

"Pyroengraving" is one method used to embellish gourds. With this technique, a heated blade is used to burn lines into the surface. Sometimes the surface is cut away, and the stripped areas are painted, dyed, or burned to add contrast. Beads or cowrie shells can also be added. Groups that decorate gourds include the Masai and Boran of Kenya and the Tonga of Mozambique. Young women in Cameroon kept decorated gourds to indicate their status; a calabash, for example, revealed her status as a mother. For a Fulani woman, decorated gourds would be part of her dowry, marking her wealth, social status, and household skills. She was likely to have gourds for special occasions as well as everyday vessels.

While in many parts of the continent artisans, including weavers, could be of either sex, potters were generally female, whereas blacksmiths and woodcarvers were male. Blacksmiths have always been held in high regard in Africa, partly because of the importance placed on their ability to make such valuable items as coins, tools, instruments, and weapons. Their cultural imprint is evidenced in the many gates and other wrought-iron works that bear religious symbols.

OPPOSITE: Photographed against traditional Adinkra fabric, a collection of hand carved wooden objects expresses the creative exuberance of West African designs.

128

INTEGRATING AFRICAN OBJECTS IN THE HOME

You are the curator of your home, overseeing the display of your treasured possessions. As a repository for the objects that tell your story, that evoke your memories and explain your tastes, your home might include Grandma's coverlet upon your bed to keep you warm at night or some vintage photographs of real and acquired ancestors, as well as a variety of African objects and figures.

ABOVE: Barbara Carter-Mitchell has placed a basket adorned with cowrie shells, a Dogon vessel, a rustic lamp, and carved figures on her painted Moroccan trunk.
OPPOSITE, TOP: Maureen Zarember creates a contrast between her silver tea service and the smooth glow of her amber beads.
OPPOSITE, BOTTOM: A Yoruba bag creates a simple design using beads and cowrie shells.

Incorporating this art into your home is a creative challenge, whether you are a serious collector, a passionate amateur, or a casual admirer. Not only should you take into account such factors as maintaining a visual balance among your furnishings, but you should also consider how much you really want to live with these pieces. Since African art has such strong visual and tactile allure, do you want your family and guests to be able to handle the pieces? Or do you want them to look but not touch?

Consider displaying the art on a deep windowsill or on a pedestal. Arrange similar pieces on a desk, or incorporate them into a bookcase. Don't overlook the top of an armoire or even the space beneath a table. Small items—gold weights, for example—can be placed under glass in a recessed area of a coffee table.

HOW TO BUY AFRICAN ART

Authenticity is an endlessly debated topic when it comes to African art. For some art experts, anything made by African hands is authentic. It makes no difference how much contact the artist has had with outside influences that may have tainted the "purity" of his expression, or whether his reasons for creating are aesthetic, ritual, functional, or economic. These collectors and scholars maintain that African artists have been exposed to outside influences throughout the ages, from members of other ethnic groups as well as from Arabs and Europeans. As for the possibly mercenary motives of some art, these experts also note that bartering has always influenced the work and productivity of artists.

The question to ask is, what does it mean to you? How much do you care about authenticity, a hard-to-pin-down concept? How important to you are origin, intention, rarity, quality? Must you have an original Shetani figure by Samaki Likonkoa, the Makonde carver who introduced the spirit figure in Dar-es-Salaam in the late 1950s? Or will a reasonable facsimile do?

If, as an investor or as a serious collector, you want a museum-quality collection, questions of origin and quality will clearly be of great importance. For others with less exacting standards, something short of a unique masterpiece will be sufficient. For many of us, the question then becomes, do I like it? If the answer is yes, we are satisfied, regardless of provenance.

When looking to acquire art from Africa or elsewhere, it all comes down to taste. Do your homework, so that you can become an informed consumer and collector. Read, visit museums, talk to people from various African countries, and consult with art dealers and other experts. In time, your eye for African art will grow keener, and you will learn to pick out pieces that truly bring you pleasure.

We

like things just so when it's time to drift off to sleep. We have to be on our own side of the bed, in the spot that knows our body oh so well. Some of us need to be able to hear a pin drop in order to fall asleep, others prefer soft music, and those who really know how to rest can sleep through just about anything. When it comes to the degrees of darkness, a child may insist on a night light while an adult may want a pitch-black room. The final ingredient is

bedrooms

often a book (good or bad), a hot bath, tea, or a glass of warm milk, followed by reflective words of thanks and inspiration.

What makes these bedtime rituals so comforting and relaxing is often the setting. After all, the bedroom is our sanctuary, the one room in which we really take time for ourselves. We've learned to appreciate bedrooms even more as our lives grow busier. And with tight schedules and sometimes tight living quarters, this retreat becomes not only a place to recharge our batteries, but also a multi-purpose base for extra work, exercise, or recreation.

132

Using elements of African style can enable you to transform this very personal and private space into an oasis. The sleep rituals of Africa are fascinating and can inspire bedrooms that reflect the spirit of the continent through texture, light, color, and motifs. As they say in Burkina Faso, welcome to Zanuteg, the land of sleep!

PLACES OF REST

Like other pieces of furniture in Africa, beds vary greatly in style and form. They have ranged from simple mats or animal skins tossed on the ground to elaborately carved masterpieces passed down through generations. For nomadic groups in particular, mats are essential items representing much more than beds. These treasured possessions serve many purposes, including sleeping, sitting, and eating. Often woven tightly enough to keep out wind, rain, and sun, mats can be placed directly on the floor, but they have also been used on beds made of mud, clay, stone, or wood.

Dried-mud beds were common in areas of the continent with arid climates. Often about a foot high, they were wide enough for one or two people. Deluxe models were hollow rather than solid so that a fire could be set under the platform to keep bodies warm and cozy.

In many parts of Africa, beds were carved from large chunks of wood. The Tiv of Nigeria and the Senufo of the Ivory Coast were among the groups known for their wooden beds. Some beds were carved with a variety of images, including spiders, which represented the connection between humans and spirits; fertility symbols to ensure procreation and longevity; or cowrie shells, a sign of wealth. The Tiv treasured these beds and carefully preserved them as heirlooms. They even had a saying about a child being conceived on a *kpande*, as the solid wooden bed was known: a reference to a kpande was a sign of legitimacy.

In Egypt, beds often had carved legs and feet representing animals. Embellished at times with ivory or gold and other precious metals, some were also enlivened with paint. These beds had footboards, but no headboards, since they were often built on a slant with the head resting higher than the feet.

Other variations on the wooden bed involved placing forked sticks in the ground and binding poles to them to create a frame. This type of bed was popular in coastal regions and rain forests, where poles were made of raffia ribs or saplings; the Dagara people of Burkina Faso, for example, used sturdy strips of wood from the yila tree to create their supports.

PREVIOUS PAGE: When Robert Teszar came across this massively proportioned Senufo bed from the Ivory Coast, the Manhattan stylist and set decorator knew that it was for him. It doubles as a chaise and sofa for guests, and shows off the intricately embroidered patterns of Teszar's traditional Hungarian textiles and his Kasai woven velvet from Zaire. Other design elements include an East African spear and a rich Middle Eastern carpet.

OPPOSITE TOP: Incorporating an assortment of furnishings, this attic room at the top of Drs. Kariamu and Molefe Welsh-Asante's home is an exotic retreat. A Senufo hand-carved door from the Ivory Coast serves as the headboard for a bed that is covered with an Akan striped textile from Ghana; the duvet and sheets from Revman Textiles are inspired by West African design. The mortar and pestle are also from Ghana, while the two-piece king's chair is by the Showa of Zimbabwe.

BOTTOM, LEFT: This detail of the hand-carved lock of the Senufo door reveals that even the smallest detail is a work of art. Plump pillows—one a royal blue and one with a West African print—provide comfort and color.

BOTTOM, RIGHT: The elaborately carved king's chair in the Welsh-Asantes' attic opens and closes like a deck chair: the seat, which feeds through an opening in the back, is removable.

generally curved, the base was straight, and the supports between the two areas often bear the detailed craftsmanship that makes headrests coveted items for collectors.

SLEEPING CUSTOMS

As with all activities of daily life, sleeping in Africa is accompanied by diverse customs. The orientation one might assume in bed, for example, varies widely. Among the Merina of Madagascar, the northeast is a hallowed direction, and so to pay honor to the family ancestors, a Merina patriarch will sleep with his head toward the northeast. Others in the residence who are deemed less important are oriented to the south and west. On the other hand, the Tiv of Nigeria simply place the head of their beds toward the door and the foot in the direction of the wall. Among the Afar people in Ethiopia, a man sleeps on his right side on top of his right hand, while a woman sleeps on the left side of her body and uses her right hand to touch her spouse.

The bed has also been considered important as a means of smooth passage into the next life. In coastal Zaire, for example, the Yombe try to ensure that the last rest is a comfortable one by putting beds on top of graves. The Senufo swaddled the bodies of their dead in fabric and placed them on beautifully carved wooden beds for viewing and mourning. And in eastern Nigeria, the burial chambers of leaders were lined with mats for their sleeping comfort.

In keeping with Africa's rich oral tradition, bedtime stories are an important part of the nighttime ritual as well. Besides being entertaining, these stories carried instructive messages and kept a village's history and traditions alive; many of the stories concerned sleep and dreams.

CREATING YOUR OWN OASIS

For those who dream of sleeping on a wooden African bed, a trip to the continent or to an art dealer is in order. Keep in mind that these traditional beds can be very heavy, since they are often carved from a large chunk of wood. It took several reluctant movers to get design stylist Robert Teszar's Senufo bed into his New York apartment. His cherished bed doubles as seating when company comes. To make it more comfortable, Teszar added padding and covered it with richly textured fabrics from Hungary and Zaire.

If you have classical tastes, follow Roger Prigent's lead. The owner

ABOVE: An Ethiopian chair carved from teak casts delicate shadows on J. R. Sanders's bedroom wall. LEFT: While quite formal in its European and Egyptian aesthetic, Roger Prigent's bedroom is nonetheless one of comfort and ease. Classical Greek columns, ornately hand-crafted furnishings and finishes, a large painting from the art nouveau period, and a plush fur combine to create a striking environment.

of Malmaison Antiques in New York, Prigent has a French Empire bed circa 1805 complete with carvings of an Egyptian woman's head on two of the four bedposts. His elegant bed makes a strong statement and complements other Egyptian elements; this regal setting also includes classical Greek columns, a large painting from the Art Nouveau period, and a collection of Empire-style accessories and toiletries on the dressing table. But if you want a one-of-a-kind look, design a bed yourself or employ a specialist who creates custom furniture. Courtney Sloane of Jersey City, New Jersey, designed a modern version of an Egyptian bed made of African ribbonwood and brushed aluminum (see page 136).

To work with what you already have, simply changing the sheets and other bed accessories can dramatically transform the look of your room, adding African style and color. Indeed, the bedroom is one of the best places to use traditional African textiles. Kente cloth can be folded at the foot of the bed to complement solid sheets or used as a blanket on chilly nights. For example, Tahira Amatullah, a textile dealer in Philadelphia, used blue-and-yellow Kente to brighten her bedroom; the colors add a feeling of warmth and intimacy to a space with pure white walls. A Matisse pillowcase behind some

RIGHT: J. R. Sanders incorporates all regions of Africa in his bedroom: the Moroccan mirror and intricately patterned lantern are North African; the teak chair is from Ethiopia; the textiles are from western Sudan; and the headboard is covered with mud cloth from Mali.

OPPOSITE: Artist Gosta Claesson brought back from a trip to Africa the indigo and white fabric used for this bedspread. He evoked its geometric patterns in the mural that frames the Louis XIII mirror.

ABOVE: Handmade African dolls from Lorrie Payne Creations of Philadelphia rest on the guest bed in Denys and Tony Davis's home until company comes. Most of the comforts of home are included in this cozy space, from the inviting tub painted with an African-inspired border to the spacious bed, covered with bed linen from Beacon Looms' Mali line.

black-and-white African textile completes the look.

You can also try covering an otherwise plain headboard with a heavy textile such as mud cloth. J. R. Sanders, who specializes in museum and interior design in New York, chose a brown-and-black mud cloth to cover his headboard and added throw pillows in a contrasting Korhogo pattern.

For a coordinated look, you can buy machine-made African textiles at a local fabric store. These fabrics are easy to care for, and the patterns are unlimited. Cover a lampshade with fabric that matches your bed, consider a fabric border along the top of the wall, or cover an unsightly bed base with a favorite pattern. Raw silk in bright blue, green, and turquoise serves as a bedspread in rug dealer Carlos Ascher's bedroom in Philadelphia, giving his room a Moroccan feel;

TOP: The Algotssons' bedroom is fresh, light, and African-inspired. The natural textiles include bedding of brushed linen and cotton, bordered by a full-length woven raffia and appliquéd dance skirt created by the Kuba of Zaire. An Asante stool from Ghana provides seating at the dressing table, while a lidded Kenyan basket offers extra storage.

BELOW: A mirror in the Algotsson bedroom reflects African-inspired motifs in more ways than one: playful designs have been painted on the wall around the mirror and the space above the bay windows.

handmade silk pillowcases embellished with tassels and a Moroccan rug at the foot of the bed are appropriate accents.

Today, bed linen manufacturers make sheets, pillowcases, bedspreads, bed skirts, curtains, and wall borders in a wide variety of African-inspired patterns and colors. For example, Denys Davis's guest bedroom sports linen from the "Mali" line by Beacon Looms. These easy-care, authentic black-and-white patterns come with a matching Kente-patterned quilt cover. Use them together, or mix and match them to create your own look. If the pattern you like is unavailable in a matching window treatment, simply drape an extra sheet over a rod to create a valance.

For a finishing touch, cover cushions in an assortment of complementing fabrics and then add African sculptures and fresh flowers.

According to one tradition, during a walk through a forest, two Asante hunters noticed a spider spinning a web. They were fascinated by its skill and marveled at how the spider turned ordinary lines into intricate patterns. Little did the spider know that it had such devoted students or that they were trying their best to duplicate its technique. Days later, the hunters returned to their village and shared the fruits of their effort with the chief, who felt their discovery was worthy of the king's attention. Osei TuTu, the Asantehene

TEXTILE TRADITION

or king of the Asante, was elated when he saw the woven strip and commissioned the men to weave this colorful silk cloth solely for his royal court. This regal fabric is known as Kente cloth, and today it is one of the most popular textiles woven on the continent of Africa.

In one form or another, weaving has played an extremely important role in the development of human history. From the earliest times, hair from the skins of hunted and domestic animals was woven to insulate and pro-

tect homes. Along with fibers from various plants and trees, it provided the means to create such necessities as bedding, clothing, wall and door hangings, and blankets. As textiles became more sophisticated, they were even used as currency for trading. Archaeological data show that the earliest remains of textiles are found in the Nile Valley from as early as 3200 B.C. Many of the ancient designs and weaving techniques are still being used today and remain an important part of African lifestyles.

Weaving techniques and fibers today vary only slightly from region to region. For example, narrow strip weaving is practiced in West Africa and is also used in Zaire, with the only difference being that Zairian weavers often incorporate raffia palm leaf to create their Kuba cloth. As is the case with other African arts, textile patterns usually have specific meanings and uses. Some textiles, for example, are woven by men, others by women, and if weavers in a given area include both men and women, they may use different types of looms. Normally handmade, these looms are handed down from generation to generation. They can be placed in horizontal, vertical, or angular positions. In North Africa, for example, women weave wool for tents, cushions, and blankets on horizontal looms, whereas both men and women use vertical looms to weave carpets.

Whether or not the fibers used in weaving are dyed beforehand, the finished textiles are often embellished through hand-stamping, stenciling, dyeing, painting, or embroidery. Paint can be made from soil, and dyes can be derived from herbs, leaves, bark, nuts, fruits, vegetables, and grasses; these are mixed with water or with naturally occurring chemicals such as zinc, sulfur, or iron to obtain the desired thickness and hue. Colors hold different cultural meanings based on village or family affiliations. In some parts of Nigeria, red is a threatening color worn by chiefs to protect them from evil, but it is a sign of accomplishment in other areas, while red is used for mourning robes by the Akan in Ghana and for burial cloths in Madagascar.

Traditionally, many African textiles were not cut or tailored. Instead, they were draped and tied to suit various uses. But with the current

OPPOSITE: Textile dealer Veronica Robertson breaks up the neutral expanse of her sofa with Ewe cloth pillows. The living room in her Manhattan loft contains an ebullient mix of textures: the sensuality of African textiles, the earthiness of terra-cotta, the solidity of wooden carvings and vessels, the organic feel of dried plants, and the intricate craftsmanship of woven Ogboni baskets.

interest in textiles outside Africa, both handmade and printed fabrics are now being cut and fashioned into contemporary clothing and home furnishings, including pillows, upholstered furniture, wall hangings, blankets, and throws. And their patterns have been replicated for use on other products as well, from sneakers and plastic shower curtains to plates and ice buckets.

African and African-inspired textiles can be used in a variety of ways. Authentic textiles work well as throws or even bedspreads if you really want to live with the pieces. When textiles are fragile or rare, consider having them professionally mounted or framed for use as wall hangings. Machine-made fabrics and reproductions are best for uses that involve heavy wear and tear, such as pillows, curtains, upholstered furniture, and the like. They achieve the look of African style with a bonus of durability.

RIGHT: This Ghanaian silk Ewe wall hanging is from the collection of Berry Ann Boxley. The pattern, woven by men, represents freedom, knowledge, and unity. The leather chair is covered with a Zairian woven raffia skirt.

OPPOSITE: A 19th-century Swedish kitchen sofa is covered with a variety of contemporary African prints. The metal marionettes were designed by Robert Phillips.

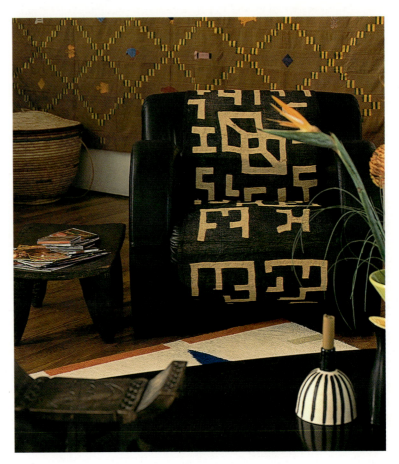

TREASURED TEXTILES

This guide to textiles and techniques represents just a few of the most popular styles of African fabric. Available throughout the world from galleries, boutiques, and fabric stores, their striking colors and patterns also inspire many artists and designers.

ADINKRA (top): According to the folklore associated with this cloth, a king known as Adinkra boasted of having a golden stool similar to the sacred stool of the Asante. The Asante were angered and waged a war with the king, who was killed in the battle. His son was then abducted and forced to teach the Asante about hand-stamping on fabric. Adinkra means "farewell" and was used for funerals and to bid a formal farewell to guests. Dark colors, like brick red, brown, or black, were associated with death, while white, yellow, and light blue were worn for festive occasions. Adinkra is made by embroidering wide panels of dyed cotton and then stamping them with carved calabash symbols. The tarlike resin used for these designs is obtained from the boiled bark of the badia tree after it has been mixed with iron slag. Adinkra patterns are numerous, ranging from crescents to abstract forms; each symbol carries its own significance and represents events of daily life. The cloth is still produced in Ghana.

ADIRE (bottom): This indigo resist-dyed cloth comes from Nigeria ("adire" is a Yoruba word) and is made from plain cotton. There are two types of Adire. One is made by tie-dying or by stitching a design with raffia; this is known as *Adire Oniko*. With the second method, *Adire Eleko*, a design is painted freehand or stenciled using a starchy paste made from cassava or yams. Both techniques allow cloth to resist

indigo when submerged into dye pits, resulting in a wide range of patterns. Of the two, Adire Oniko is more commonly found today. Both styles are available in a variety of geographical and representational motifs.

APPLIQUÉ (top): Technically, appliqué is a textile art, rather than a form of weaving. Indigenous to Africa, appliqué is practiced by the Fante of Ghana, the Fon people of Benin, and the Egyptians. Typically, colors are true to life, based on the item being represented, with scenes drawn from history, myths, or personal experiences; Egyptian appliqués feature stunning geometric designs. Great care is taken in sizing and choosing the appropriate background and forms. Beads, shells, and other materials are sometimes used to further embellish the cloth. Most often, these vividly colored cloths were fashioned into banners, flags, or umbrellas.

ASOKE (bottom): Although this cloth is sturdy and practical, the Yoruba in Nigeria did not use it for everyday use; it was reserved for funerals, religious rituals, and other formal occasions. Woven in 4-inch-wide strips that vary in length, Asoke today is most often spun by hand or machine in cotton intermingled with Lurex (metallic) and rayon threads; it can also be commissioned in silk threads. The older Asoke fabrics include indigo ikat-dyed warp threads that create a striped pattern. Some older cloths are also characterized by their openwork or holes. Asoke is noted for its supplementary inlays, which are generally made of rayon threads on a background of silk cotton.

BATIK (next page, top): To create the popular batik cloths, patterns are made by applying melted wax on the fabric—usually cotton—so that those areas will resist color when submerged in a dye bath. The first step is to wash the cotton fabric to remove its sizing. Then a design is lightly drawn onto the surface. For multicolored effects, colors are applied one on top of the other, beginning with the lightest hue. Wax is applied as each color is added to keep them from colliding and to create the pattern. After the cloth is dyed yellow, for example, melted wax is applied in those areas that will remain yellow. The cloth is dried after each stage of the dyeing process, and then the wax is removed by scraping and sometimes boiling it off.

EMBROIDERY: Cloths displaying this textile art can be found throughout Africa. Typically, patterns are drawn onto the fabric and then it is stitched by hand or by machine in a complementary color of thread. The embroidered patterns often convey special meanings. Most often found on tunics, pants, and other articles of clothing, embroidery is also stitched on unfinished cloth, which can be displayed as wall hangings or used to make a variety of decorative items for the home.

EWE (bottom): The style of this cloth is similar to that of the Asantes' Kente. Named for the Ewe people, who originate from the southeastern region of Ghana, it basically comes in two types. People of wealth wear the first type, which is often commissioned and elaborately decorated. Made of silk, rayon, or cotton, this cloth typically contains inlays of symbols representing knowledge, ethics, and morals as applied to daily life. The second type is a more commercial cloth made from simple cotton fibers and featuring modest patterns. These humbler cloths sometimes contain smaller, simpler versions of the more elaborate designs, but they always have a beauty of their own.

IKAT: Found throughout Africa, this textile is tie-dyed in one color such as indigo or in a variety of colors. The cloth is stitched or tied so that the dye will not penetrate other areas. Although

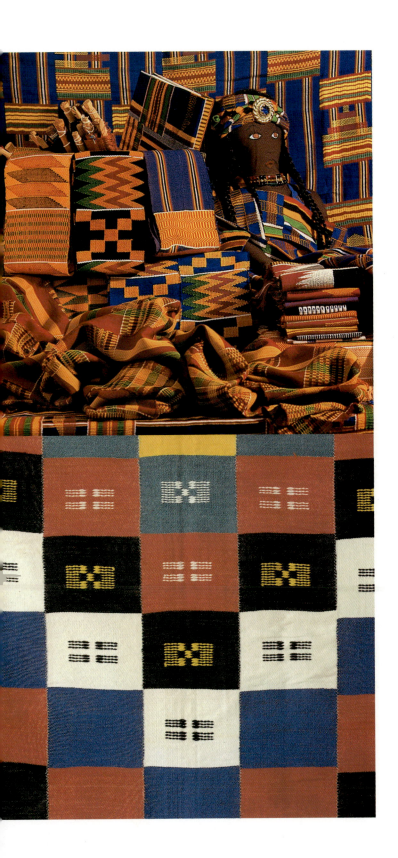

patterns are unlimited, some Ikat cloths feature symbols of the moon and stars, while others have circular designs, which tend to be easier to make. The patterns are typically for decoration and carry no special religious significance.

KENTE (top): Folklore links Kente to the Asante hunters' encounter with the spider or Anansi. But the word "Kente" is said to have originated from the Fante people of Ghana, who sold this cloth and carried it in baskets—the Fante word for basket is "kenten." Authentic Kente is woven in 4-inch-wide strips. Large pieces are made by sewing the strips together along the selvage; although now often done by machine, the traditional method is to whipstitch the segments by hand. Machine-sewn Kente generally has a zigzag stitch or, rarely, a straight stitch. Kente patterns have religious, political, and even financial significance. Today, there's a pattern to mark the importance of almost any special occasion, and colors are chosen to reflect customs and beliefs. Red represents death or bloodshed, and is often worn during political rallies; green stands for fertility and vitality, and is worn by girls during puberty rites; white means purity or victory; yellow represents glory and maturity and is worn by chiefs; gold, for continuous life, is also worn by chiefs; blue, for love, is often worn by the queen mother; and black, meaning aging and maturity, is used to signify spirituality. Because of its vibrant beauty and regal legacy as a cloth fit for kings and queens, authentic Kente remains one of the most popular fabrics on the market.

KHASA (bottom): These heavy woolen striped blankets are woven by the Fulani of Mali. Approximately 6 to 8 feet long, they are woven in 8-inch-wide strips, with the strips sewn together to create each blanket. Although the traditional blanket is usually all white, it nevertheless has a striped effect because of the different weaving techniques used for the alternating pieces, creating gradations in hue. Made to order for the cold season, the blankets are also found with yellow, black, or red stripes.

KORHOGO (top): This handspun cloth, made by the Senufo people of the Ivory Coast, is the same as that used for mud cloth (see below), with the designs applied in a similar fashion. To make wide pieces of Korhogo cloth, handwoven cotton strips roughly 5 inches wide are sewn together at the selvage. Mud is painted on the finished cloth to create patterns of animals, men in ceremonial dress, buildings, or geometric designs. The soil used to make this mud paint is generally black, brown, or rust and is collected throughout the region. The cloth, which comes in various lengths and widths, is used for clothing as well as for pillows, wall hangings, and folding screens.

KUBA (bottom): Indigenous to Zaire, this textile is tightly woven using strands from raffia palm leaves for both warp and weft. Raffia strands are also interwoven between the warp and weft to create intricate geometric patterns. Kuba cloth comes in essentially two forms. One has a rich, velvety pile; the other has a flat weave with little or no pile. For both, vegetable dyes are used on raffia threads that are then embroidered onto finished cloth to create patterns; these rectangles, lines, creative curvatures, and circles all have special meanings. Appliqué is another technique used to create Kuba patterns. Panels and strips of Kuba are sewn together to make larger pieces of cloth, which is used for ceremonial skirts, wall hangings, or mats for sitting and sleeping.

MANJAKA (next page, top): It's unlikely that you'll find a solid block of color anywhere on Manjaka cloth, which is distinguished by its intricate geometric patterns. Made from cotton in

Guinea-Bissau, the fabric has such detailed patterns that weavers often need assistants to help them with the complex designs. If a piece of Manjaka cloth has triangles, for example, the background area will also feature a pattern—perhaps tighter and smaller. Woven in 7-inch-wide strips that are sewn together, Manjaka cloth was once traded throughout Africa and Europe.

MUD CLOTH (bottom): Originating from Mali and once worn by hunters in the region, mud cloth is made from narrow strips of hand-spun and handwoven cotton, which are sewn together in various widths and lengths. The cloth is first dyed with a yellow solution extracted from the bark of the M'Peku tree and the leaves and stems of the wolo tree; the solution acts as a mordant or fixative. Then, using carved bamboo or wooden sticks, symbolic designs are applied in mud that has been collected from riverbanks and allowed to ferment over time. After the mud is applied to the cloth, it is dried in the sun. The process is repeated several times to obtain a rich color that is deeply imbued in the cloth. When it reaches the desired hue, the cloth is washed with a caustic solution to remove debris and to brighten the background. Today, mud cloth comes in background shades of white, yellow, rich brown, light brown, and rust; the example shown here is called bogolanfini.

PAKHAMANI: This is a Zulu word that means "uplifting oneself." Pakhamani textiles are created by women in South Africa, displaying designs full of personal significance. The women use brushes to apply dyes mixed with sorghum paste to cotton. Then they bake the fabric at high temperatures and scrape off the paste. The process is repeated for each color, resulting in vibrant patterns with geometric symbols, animals, flowers, and other images.

CARE AND CLEANING

Special care is required to maintain and preserve African textiles. Because the traditional cloths are made from natural materials, moths, carpet beetles, silverfish, rodents, mold, and mildew can damage these beautiful fibers, while textiles that are exposed to the air—wall hangings, for example—attract dust particles.

One way to remove this buildup is to lay the textile flat and dust it with a low-powered hand-held vacuum cleaner. Textiles that are colorfast and in good condition can be cleaned with a solution of mild soap and soft, warm water. However, to avoid damage, never agitate the cloth; simply let the bath do the work. For heavier stains, rinse and repeat the process.

Some textiles can also be dry-cleaned, but cleaning solutions are often too harsh on the fibers and can wear them out. Creases and wrinkles can be removed from clean textiles by steaming; always check the steam machine instructions before using.

Care should also be taken in storing textiles, which should be clean when put away. Avoid creasing the fabric, which can cause stress and damage to the fibers. Place rolls of acid-free paper along the folds, and store flat in a drawer that will not tarnish, rust, or break down the fibers. Keep in mind that these fibers are fragile. Avoid unnecessary pressure, and never place heavier fabrics or weighty objects on top of the textiles. Consult a textile expert for rare, fragile, or old textiles or if you're concerned about storage and cleaning.

OPPOSITE: This colorful stack comprises four-inch-wide strips of traditional Kente patterns, handwoven of 100 percent rayon.
ABOVE: Kahso cloth from Burkina Faso is used to cover tent walls.

A herd of antelope roaming the high savanna plains. Flocks of exotic birds flying against an opaline sky. Crocodiles and hippos sharing a drink of water at the edge of a river. Rays of sunlight filtering through a canopy of foliage. These are images of Africa in all its beauty.

Nature provides much of the symbolism found in African style. Visual and tactile design cues emerge from the landscapes, animal life, and vegetation that

outdoor spaces

can be found from the northern edge of Africa to the Cape of Good Hope in the south. Inspiration can come from the snow-capped peaks of Kilimanjaro, the dense forests or tropical jungles, the dusty hues of the simmering Sahara, or the rich bounty of the Gold Coast.

The environment also determines the materials artisans might use: rosewood or African walnut, clay or soapstone, bamboo or raffia. In the equatorial forests, for example, baobab and ebony trees are

160

PRECEDING PAGE: Drs. Kariamu and Molefe Welsh-Asante surround themselves with African art in their outdoor living space. Ghanaian Kente printed cushions and Nigerian textiles complement the lush foliage. The mask on the tree is a reproduction of an Ife female deity from Nigeria.

OPPOSITE: This metal sculpture by Joe Sam is his interpretation of a slave ship.

RIGHT: Warren Robbins has placed a pair of sculptures from Benin in his garden. The pieces represent gods from West African mythology.

BELOW: This is an example of a popular side table found in Moroccan markets. It has a wrought-iron base and a stone tabletop covered with ceramic tiles.

abundant. A magnificent tree that can grow up to 60 feet tall with a trunk up to 50 feet in diameter, the baobab's fibers can be used to make cloth, rope, and paper, while the ebony tree provides the hard, dark wood often used in making furniture, veneers, and sculpture. In the northern region, materials include cork, oak, eucalyptus, and papyrus. The Egyptians, of course, learned how to make paper from the stalk of the papyrus plant and rope from its fibers. They also made baskets, mats, and sandals from this tall reed plant, native to the banks of the Nile River.

Studying how nature works—how birds build nests, say, or how spiders weave webs—influenced techniques for weaving, building houses, and even caring for the young. Egyptians, for example, designed homes to best harmonize with their environment. Rooms were oriented to catch the evening breezes, and beautiful hanging gardens were incorporated to add colors and perfumes to the home.

Perhaps the most common, and at times most overused, source of natural inspiration comes from Africa's animal kingdom. The beauty of lions, panthers, leopards, tigers, and zebras has captivated people the world over. Fashion designers use leopard prints in everything from

coats to shoes, and animal patterns—real and reproduced—have always been favorites of interior designers for pillows, rugs, and upholstery. Wood carvings of elephants, rhinoceroses, and giraffes abound; ostrich feathers and eggs are used for decoration; antelopes, elephants, and other animals are hunted for their horns and tusks. Visit any zoo and the attraction to Africa's animals is as much on display as they are. So strong is the call of the wild that tourists spend huge sums of money each year to go on safari and get up close to these animals in their natural environment.

OPPOSITE: In creating her outdoor space, Margreet Monster draws upon the imagery of Morocco, with an emphasis on color, pattern, and form. Her design includes intense blues and pinks with a splash of turquoise; stripes and busy geometrics; lots of pillows and cushions; recycled glass and North African ceramics; and flowers indigenous to Africa such as geraniums, impatiens, and lilies. The slate slabs come together to form a geometrically patterned floor that anchors and defines the borders of her outdoor room. **LEFT:** Monster's vintage wicker rocking chair has a pyramid back and is very much in tune with her colorful pillows and Moroccan pottery.

AFRICA IN YOUR BACKYARD

Since so much of its imagery is derived from nature and relates intimately to outdoor settings, bringing African elements to the area surrounding your own home is a powerful way to establish a visual link to the continent. You can add lush African vegetation, wooden or metal objects, masks, and figures. Consider using sisal for patio floors and other surfaces. Experiment with African textiles for table linens and chair cushions as well as for pillows or mats that can be used for sitting around a low table. Serve food from real calabashes, and place

African sculptures on the table as the centerpiece. You might also take a cue from the Ndebele of South Africa, who paint the outside of their houses in colorful geometric patterns. An adaptation might be just the thing for an architectural detail or even a piece of furniture.

The Welsh-Asantes of Philadelphia live with the look and feel of Africa inside and out: this aesthetic flows naturally from their interiors to their backyard patio and garden. Lush greenery surrounds the area. The patio's wicker sofa is covered with a machine-made Kente cloth, which adds a vibrant warmth. The table is dressed with a batik fabric, while African baskets hold the feast. This patio looks and feels as if the guests were picnicking in the middle of an African rain forest.

"It is important for the soul to always be close to nature," says Margreet Monster, a landscape architect in Philadelphia, and she has ensured this in her outdoor garden. There, nature gets a boost with indigenous plants from Africa including agapanthus, or lily of the Nile, from Egypt and clivia from South Africa. Rich North African colors such as hot pink and deep blues cover the cushion on her wooden bench. A wrought-iron Moroccan gate adds a rustic feel to the other accessories that surround it. Relaxation comes naturally in this garden.

In establishing the same effect in your own garden, keep in mind that everything you use outdoors must obviously defy the elements, withstanding sun, heat, rain, and wind. Some pieces of sculpture do weather well or acquire a patina that adds a richness to their appeal. And certainly include plants and flowers that are indigenous to Africa. Here is a list of the more common African plants available in nurseries throughout the world:

AFRICAN IRIS: These white and yellow flowers have swordlike leaves. Their blooms last only a day and their petals turn blue when they die.

AFRICAN VIOLET: This popular flower with the little yellow centers hails from the hills of Kenya. It ranges in hue from pink to purple.

AGAPANTHUS: Better known as the lily of the Nile, this tubular flower can be pure white or deep blue. It is ideal for cuttings.

ALOE: Ancient Egyptians used this member of the lily family to heal burns, to ease the sting of insect bites, and to relieve pain. Keep this plant handy at the family barbecue.

AMARYLLIS: This eye-catching plant comes in an array of colors and grows to about 2 feet in height. It also works well as a potted plant.

BLACK-EYED SUSAN: A common climbing plant, this vine grows up to 10 feet in length or more. Orange, red, pink, or white flowers encircle the black center.

OPPOSITE, clockwise from top left: An African orchid; an African violet; a Calla lily; and an amaryllis. These lovely flowering plants are only a few of the many species originally indigenous to the African continent that have now become so familiar to our gardens and homes.

CALLA LILY: This fragrant funnel-shaped flower grows wild in Africa and can be eaten as a vegetable. Hybrids come in gold, red, or pink.

EUPATORIUM: Also known as the mist flower, this exotic plant has fluffy violet flowers and heart-shaped green leaves.

HIBISCUS: This flower grows wild in Kenya and can remain fresh for an entire day without water. While it is typically yellow with a purple center, some hybrids are red.

IMPATIENS: This plant loves shade and is easy to grow. Its many colors include pink, orange, white, red, and lavender.

ORCHIDS: Orchids from the African continent are smaller than other varieties. Light in scent, they grow best in a fairly rainy climate.

WATER LILY: Known as the blue lotus and found in Egypt, this flower has a light scent and large tough leaves.

FESTIVALS AND OUTDOOR ACTIVITIES

One place that captures the essence of outdoor life in Africa is the marketplace. From Tunisia to South Africa, the bustling, noisy marketplace is an integral part of the African lifestyle. There, people are engrossed in buying and selling meat, fruit, vegetables, household items, baskets, and fabrics. It is a place to grab a bite to eat, socialize, and pick up the stuff of everyday life. Haggling is an art at these markets, and is expected.

The marketplace concept exists, of course, beyond the borders of Africa. Today, vendors regularly sell African and African-inspired items at indoor and outdoor markets from Harlem to Los Angeles, as well as at annual festivals. The annual summer Odunde Festival in Philadelphia, for example, celebrates the African New Year and has been in existence for twenty years. Other festivals include the African Street Festival in New York and the Carabana, which also focuses on the Caribbean, in Toronto, Canada. Like the county fairs of Middle America, these festivals and marketplaces provide links to a cultural past, where one can sample the sights, sounds, colors, and pleasures of the African experience, and are also the perfect places to buy African goods for the home at bargain prices.

OPPOSITE: Playfully decorative, this combination of traditional African rattles and contemporary plates creates a lively outdoor table.
LEFT: Even the simplest of North African elements can brighten a table.

RESOURCES

ANTIQUES

**Center for African
American Arts**
2221 Peachtree Rd.,
Suite D341
Atlanta, GA 30309
(404) 605-0734
African-American decorative arts
and antiques

Findings
246 Race St.
Philadelphia, PA 19106
(215) 923-0988
Antiques, reproductions,
collectibles

Malmaison Antiques
253 E. 74th St.
New York, NY 10021
(212) 288-7569
Egyptian Revival and Empire
furniture

Santa Kilim
401 S. Guadalupe St.
Santa Fe, NM 87501
(505) 986-0340
International antiques, artifacts, and
textiles

ARTISANS

Sweetgrass Baskets
532 E. Wimbledon Dr.
Charleston, SC 29412
(803) 722-4810

ARTS AND CRAFTS

Amazulu
323 S. 13th St.
Philadelphia, PA 19107
(215) 627-8667
Handcrafted jewelry and gifts

Bazaar Tangiers
19C W. Bridge St.
New Hope, PA 18938
(215) 862-3229
African arts and crafts

Cheryl Sutton and Associates
130 Morningside Ave.
Gary, IN 46408
(219) 981-3991
National art dealers and
consultants

Out of Africa
626 South St.
Philadelphia, PA 19147
(215) 574-9838
African arts and crafts
or
3641 Magazine St.
New Orleans, LA
(504) 945-9115

Peter Adler
191 Sussex Gardens
London, England W2
07126211775
African stools and traditional
African art

Stiltwalkers
802 South St.
Philadelphia, PA 19147
(215) 925-1677
African art and collectible artifacts

Suli Suli
Unit 1 253 Portobello Rd.
London, England W11 1LR
0712433130
Traditional African art and textiles

Window to Africa
5210 S. Harper Ct.
Chicago, IL 60615
(312) 955-7742
Traditional African art, crafts, and
fashion

CRAFTSPEOPLE AND ARTISANS

Faux Fax
314 Brown St.
Philadelphia, PA 19123
(215) 829-1299 or 923-6044
Decorative painted finishes

Joan Harrington
168 Percy Court
Norristown, PA 19401-1862
(610) 278-1627
Ceramic pottery and papers

Lorrie Payne Creations
Philadelphia, PA
(215) 923-9203
Hand-crafted dolls

Robert Phillips
221 Poplar St.
Philadelphia, PA 19123
(215) 923-6044
Custom metal furnishings,
accessories

CUSTOM FURNITURE AND INTERIOR DESIGN

Afuture
241 Ave. of the Americas
New York, NY 10014
(212) 724-7631
Custom furniture design

Alternative Design
334 Barrow St.
Jersey City, NJ 07302
(201) 413-0094
Custom design and interiors

Deborah Johnson
1801 W. Chew Ave.
Philadelphia, PA 19141
(215) 549-9156
Interior decorator

Giovanni Massaglia
315 Ninth Ave.
Haddon Heights, NJ 08035
(609) 546-0460
Tables of inlaid woods

Inside Design
1245 Medary Ave.
Philadelphia, PA 19141
(215) 224-7808
Interior and set design

Peter Pierobon
1102 E. Columbia Ave.
Philadelphia, PA 19125
(215) 425-0225
Custom furniture design

Rhonda A. Roman Interiors
2148 Seminole
Detroit, MI 48214
(313) 924-6877
Commercial and residential interiors

Right Angle Design
829 Shrader St.
San Francisco, CA 94117
(415) 386-7828
Custom furniture

Sanders Design Works
28 W. 38th St.
New York, NY 10018
(212) 921-1118
Interiors and exhibits

DECORATIVE TILES

Cerrillos Ceramics
310 W. Mt. Pleasant
Philadelphia, PA 19119
(215) 248-7974 or 487-1668
Hand-painted ceramic tiles

Charles Tiles
4401 Main St.
Manayunk, Philadelphia, PA 19127
(215) 482-8440
Decorative tiles

FLOOR COVERINGS

Tufenkian Import-Export
902 Broadway, 2nd floor
New York, NY 10010-6002
(212) 475-2475
Custom African-inspired handwoven carpets

GALLERIES AND MUSEUMS

Afro-American Historical and Cultural Museum
701 Arch St.
Philadelphia, PA 19106
(215) 574-0380
African-American arts and culture center

Alit Ash Kebede Fine Art
964 N. La Brea Ave.
Los Angeles, CA 90038
(213) 874-6269
Fine African and African-American art

Bomani Gallery
251 Post St.
San Francisco, CA 94108
(415) 296-8677
International and decorative art

Craft Caravan
63 Greene St.
New York, NY 10012
(212) 431-6669
Traditional African art, textiles, and objects

Eric Robertson African Arts
36 W. 22nd St.
New York, NY 10010
(212) 675-4045
Traditional African art

Gallerie Noir D'Ivoire
19 Rue Mazarine
Paris, France 75006
43 54 97 66
Traditional African art

Indigo Arts
153 N. Third St.
Philadelphia, PA 19106
(215) 922-4041
Ethnographic, folk, and
contemporary art

J.P. Willborg
Sibyllegatan 41
114.42 Stockholm Sweden
087830265
Antique rugs, textiles, and African
art

Lithos' Gallery
6301 Bdelmar
St. Louis, MO 63130
(314) 862-0674
Traditional African art and African-
American art

Monbrison
2, Rue des Beaux Arts
Paris, France 75006
46 34 05 20

Musee Dapper
50, Rue Victor Hugo
Paris, France 75116
45 00 01 50
Traditional African art

The Museum for African Art
593 Broadway
New York, NY 10012
(212) 966-1313
Traditional and contemporary
African art

**National Afro-American Museum
& Cultural Center**
1350 Brush Row Road
Wilberforce, OH 45384
(513) 376-4944
African-American and African art

Porter Randall Gallery
5624 La Jolla Blvd.
La Jolla, CA 92037
(619) 551-8884
African Art

Richard Presha
Philadelphia, PA
(215) 232-3622
Modern furniture

**Robbins Center for Cross-
Cultural Communication**
530 Sixth St. SE
Washington, DC 20003
African arts and informational
center

Tambaran Gallery
20 E. 76th St.
New York, NY 10021
(212) 570-0655
Traditional African and
Oceanic art

Ty Martin
2289 Fifth Ave.
New York, NY 10037
(212) 690-3756
African masks and sculpture

William Karg
330 W. 108th St.
New York, NY 10025
(212) 662-8799
Contemporary African art

HOME FURNISHINGS AND ACCESSORIES

ABC Carpet and Home
888 Broadway
New York, NY 10003
(212) 473-3000
Carpets, antiques, and furnishings

African Home Inc.
297 Decatur St.
Brooklyn, NY 11233
(718) 363-1159
African-inspired home
accessories

Anthropologie
201 W. Lancaster Ave.
Wayne, PA 19087
(610) 687-4141
Home accessories

Cobweb
116 W. Houston St.
New York, NY 10012
(212) 505-1558
Moroccan and Egyptian furnishings

Ethan Allen
1616 Lancaster Pike
Paoli, PA 19301
(610) 644-2200

Fillamento
2185 Fillmore St.
San Francisco, CA 94115
(415) 931-2224
Furnishings and accessories

Herman Miller Inc.
855 E. Main Ave.
Zeeland, MI 49464-0302
(616) 654-3000
Eames and early modern design

The Home Zone
56 N. Third St.
Philadelphia, PA 19406
(215) 592-4215
Home accessories

IKEA
Plymouth Meeting Mall
Plymouth Meeting, PA 19462
(610) 834-0150
Furnishings and accessories

J. C. Penney
160 N. Gulph Rd.
King of Prussia, PA 19406
(610) 992-1096
Home textiles and accessories

Lumiere
112 N. Third St.
Philadelphia, PA 19106
(215) 922-6908
20th-century furniture and
accessories

OLC
152-154 N. Third St.
Philadelphia, PA 19106-1814
(215) 923-6085
Modern furniture and lighting

LIGHTING
Galbraith Paper Co.
307 N. Third St.
Philadelphia, PA 19106
(215) 923-4632
Lamps with handmade paper
shades, home textiles

Leucos USA
70 Campus Plaza II
Edison, NJ 08837
(908) 225-0010
Lighting and accessories

Resolute
1013 Stewart St.
Seattle, WA 98101-1418
(206) 343-9323
Lamps and lighting

TABLE ACCESSORIES
Chateau X
250 Mercer St.
New York, NY 10012
(212) 477-3123
Table accessories of organic
materials

Sakura
41 Madison Ave.
New York, NY 10010
(212) 683-4000
Tableware, china

Sasaki
41 Madison Ave., 13th floor
New York, NY 10010
(212) 686-5080
Tableware, flatware, and crystal

Swid Powell Design
55 W. 13th St.
New York, NY 10011
(212) 633-6699
China, silver, and crystal

TEXTILES
A & J Fabrics
752 S. Fourth St.
Philadelphia, PA 19147
(215) 592-7011
Traditional and African-inspired
textiles

Beacon Looms Inc.
295 Fifth Ave.
New York, NY 10016
(212) 685-5800
Home textiles

Handmasters
5555 Germantown Ave.
Philadelphia, PA 19144
(215) 884-8898
Traditional and contemporary
textiles

Kimberly House Ltd.
120 W. 86th St.
New York, NY 10024
(212) 977-6907
South African textiles

LFS Enterprises
for Wonoo Ventures, Ltd.
1657 The Fairway, Suite 150
Jenkintown, PA 19056
(215) 782-8489
Traditional Ghanaian Kente cloth,
stools

Motherland Interior Design
Philadelphia, PA
(215) 844-4886 or 247-7718
Custom textile design

Quilters of the Round Table
5038 Hazel Ave.
Philadelphia, PA 19143
(215) 748-5022
African-American quilts

Revman Industries Inc.
1211 Ave. of the Americas
New York, NY 10036
(212) 840-7780
Bedding, home textiles

Savanna Weave
448 W. 37th St.
New York, NY 10018
(212) 594-5227
Traditional African textiles

BIBLIOGRAPHY

Changuion, Paul. *The African Mural.* London: New Holland, 1989.

Courtney-Clark, Margaret. *African Canvas: The Art of West African Women.* New York: Rizzoli International, 1990.

———. *Ndebele: The Art of an African Tribe.* New York: Rizzoli International, 1986.

Fisher, Angela. *Africa Adorned.* New York: Harry N. Abrams, 1984.

Garner, Philippe. *Twentieth Century Furniture.* New York: Van Nostrand Reinhold, 1980.

Ketchum, William C., Jr. *Furniture 2: Neoclassic to the Present.* New York: Cooper-Hewett Museum, 1981.

Landt, Dennis, and Lisl Landt. *Morocco: Design from Casablanca to Marrakesh.* New York: Clarkson Potter, 1992.

Lucie-Smith, Edward. *Furniture: A Concise History.* New York/Toronto: Oxford University Press, 1979.

Mayberry-Lewis, David. *Millennium: Tribal Wisdom and the Modern World.* New York: Viking Penguin, 1992.

Parrender, Geoffrey. *African Mythology.* London: Hamlyn Publishing Group, 1967.

Picton, John, and John Mack. *African Textiles.* London: British Museum Publications, 1989.

Polakoff, Claire. *African Textiles and Dyeing Techniques.* London: Routledge and Kegan Paul, 1982.

Robbins, Warren M., and Nancy Nooter Ingram. *African Art in American Collections.* Washington/London: Smithsonian Press, 1989.

Welsh-Asante, Kariamu. *The African Aesthetic.* Westport, Conn.: Greenwood Press, 1993.

Williams, Geoffrey. *African Designs from Traditional Sources.* New York: Dover Publications, 1971.

Willborg, Peter. *Textiles from Five Centuries.* Stockholm: J.P. Willborg Publications, 1995.

INDEX

index

Photograph Credits

All of the photographs in this book are by George Ross except for the following: Christer Algotsson—pages 13 (top left), 116 (bottom); Bachman/Camerique—page 116 (top right); Tom Brummett—page 91; Bob McCarthy—pages 6, 10, 14 (center, top right, bottom right), 15 (bottom center,bottom right), 36 (center), 37 (left and right), 146 (right), 147 (bottom right); Rick Cadan—page 96; Solvi dos Santos—pages 14 (far left), 141; Pieter Estersohn—pages 83 (right), 93; Oberto Gili—pages 40, 42, 46; Ahmad Kenya—pages 16 (bottom right), 36 (left); Courtesy of the Metropolitan Museum of Art—page 92; Courtesy of Herman Miller Inc.—page 82 (top); Courtesy of the National African Art Museum/Smithsonian—pages 85 (top and bottom), 88; Courtesy of Cheryl Riley—pages 90 (top), 94, 97, 98, 99, 136; Courtesy of Sotheby's—page 95